The Government Inspector

Nikolai Gogol was born in Sorochintsky in the Ukraine in 1809. After a brief spell in the government service in St Petersburg, he won fame as a short story writer, and in 1836 his satirical comedy *The Government Inspector* created such a furore that he left Russia to settle in Rome, in self-imposed exile. *Marriage*, revised from an earlier draft titled *The Suitors*, was first performed in 1842, and *The Gamblers*, Gogol's only other completed play, was premiered in 1843. Gogol published the first part of his great picaresque novel *Dead Souls* in 1842, but religious mania in his latter years caused him to destroy its sequel and contributed to his early death in Moscow in 1852.

Adrian Mitchell was born in London in 1932 and went to Christchurch, Oxford. His original stage shows include *Tyger, Man Friday, Mind Your Head, White Suit Blues, A Seventh Man, In the Unlikely Event of an Emergency, Hoagy, Bix & Wolfgang Beethoven Bunkhause* and *Anna on Anna*. His adaptations of foreign plays include *Marat/Sade, The Mayor of Zalamea, Life's a Dream, The Criminals, Lost in a Mirror* and *Fuente Ovejuna*. In addition, he has written libretti, novels, books of poetry, plays for children and plays for television and radio.

THE GOVERNMENT INSPECTOR

Nikolai Gogol

Adapted by
Adrian Mitchell

Methuen Drama

Methuen 2001

2 4 6 8 10 9 7 5 3

First published in Great Britain in 1985 by
Methuen London Limited

Reissued with a new cover in 2001 by
Methuen Publishing Limited,
215 Vauxhall Bridge Road, London SW1V 1EJ

Copyright © 1985 by Adrian Mitchell

Methuen Publishing Limited Reg. No. 3543167

A CIP catalogue record for this book
is available from the British Library

ISBN 0 413 58470 4

Typeset by Deltatype Ltd, Birkenhead
Printed and bound in Great Britain by
Cox and Wyman Ltd, Reading, Berkshire

Caution

Characters and Costumes

The Governor. He is a Police Governor rather than a
mayor and has considerable power. No longer young, he is
far from being a fool. He accepts bribes, but with dignity.
He is quite a serious person, even something of a moralist.
He speaks not too loud, not too soft, not too much, not too
little. Every word he utters carries weight. His features are
coarse and hard, as are those of any official who has
worked his way up from the bottom in a demanding
service. His expression changes rapidly from fear to joy, for
he's a rough-edged character. He is normally dressed in a
frock-coat with button-holes, wears spurred jack-boots. His
hair his short and grizzled.

Anna, his wife, is a provincial coquette, not yet old. Her
education has been divided between novels and scrapbooks
and she is also very concerned with her pantry and the
servants. She is extremely inquisitive and, when the
occasion arises, displays her vanity. Now and then she gets
the better of her husband, because he can't answer back
straight away. But this happens only on trivial subjects and
on these she lectures him and sneers at him. She has four
complete changes of costume during the play.

Khlestakov. A young man of about twenty-three, slender,
rather silly and gormless – one of those people whom office
colleagues call skivers. He speaks and behaves without any
consideration for anything or anybody. He's quite incapable
of giving his whole attention to any single idea. His speech
is convulsive and words jerk out quite unexpectedly. The
more simple and ingenuous the actor in this part can be,
the better. He dresses fashionably.

Osip, Khlestakov's servant. A typical ageing servant. He
speaks seriously, eyes usually downcast – a moralizer who
likes to preach sermons to his master when his master isn't
there. His voice is always even. When he talks to his
master he takes on a strict, rough and even slightly rude

tone. He is more intelligent than his master and therefore grasps things more rapidly, but does not like to talk much and is, on the quiet, a cheat. He wears a grey or blue threadbare frock-coat.

Bobchinsky and **Dobchinsky** are both short and squat and very inquisitive. They are extraordinarily alike. Both have little paunches, both chatter at a great rate and assist their words with gestures and hand-waving. Dobchinsky is slightly taller and more serious than Bobchinsky, but Bobchinsky is jollier and livelier than Dobchinsky.

The **Judge**, Lyapkin-Tyapkin (whose name means 'higgledy-piggledy'), is a man who has read five or six books and so is slightly inclined towards freethinking. He likes to conjecture and therefore imparts a profound meaning to every word he says. The actor playing the part must keep a look of deep significance all the time. He speaks in a deep voice, drawling, wheezing, and sounds like an old clock which first hisses and then strikes.

Charity Commissioner, Zemlyanika (which means 'strawberry'), is very stout, sluggish and clumsy, but nevertheless a clever rascal. He is very obliging and fussy.

Postmaster – a man so simple that he is simply naïve.

The other parts do not call for special comment: their originals are mostly before us.

The Guests. These should be of various types. They should be tall and short, fat and thin, dishevelled and neatly-combed. Their costumes should also be varied: frockcoats, Hungarian jackets, tailcoats of all sorts of colours and cut. There should also be a great deal of variety in the women's costumes. Some are almost fashionably dressed, but always with something not quite right – either the bonnet is worn at the wrong angle or some jarring handbag is carried. Some ladies appear in dresses which don't seem to be in any conceivable fashion, with big kerchiefs, hats which look like sugar-loaves and so on.

The cast must pay special attention to the last scene. The last spoken word must have an electrifying effect on everyone simultaneously, suddenly. The whole cast must in a single instant change its position. The exclamation of astonishment must be uttered by all female characters at once, as if by a single person. If this is not properly observed, the whole effect may be lost.

Nikolai Gogol

Characters

Governor, Anton Skvoznik-Dmuchanovsky
Anna, the Governor's wife
Marya, the Governor's daughter
Schools Superintendent, Luka Khlopov
Super's Wife, Mrs Khlopov
Judge, Ammos Lyapkin-Tyapkin
Postmaster, Ivan Shpekin
Petr Dobchinsky, a landowner
Petr Bobchinsky, a landowner
Charity Commissioner, Artemy Zemlyanika
Dr Khristian (Gibner), the District Doctor
Police Inspector

Svistunov
Pugovitizin } Police Constables
Derzhimorda

Ivan Khlestakov, a Government clerk from St Petersburg
Osip, servant to Khlestakov

Ivan Rastakovsky, a retired official, respected in the
town
Stepan Korobkin, a retired official, respected in the town
Korobkin's Wife

Mishka, the Govenor's servant
Waiter at the Inn

Poshlepkinka, the Locksmith's wife
Sergeant's Widow

1st Merchant
2nd Merchant
3rd Merchant

Guests, townspeople, merchants, petitioners, serfs
The Town Band

This adaptation of *The Government Inspector* was first staged at
the National Theatre, London, in January 1985, with Rik
Mayall in the lead, directed by Richard Eyre.

Act One

Scene One

The meeting room in the **Governor**'*s house, a business-like room in which the* **Governor** *conducts his business. The* **Schools Superintendent**, *the* **Judge**, *and* **Doctor Gibner** *sit, waiting, round a table. There is a large portrait of the Czar, a slightly smaller portrait of the* **Governor** *and smaller portraits of groups sitting round the table in this same room. One chair, reserved for the* **Governor**, *and obviously more important than any of the other chairs, is empty at the head of the table. Not for long.*
   The **Governor** *strides in and stands at the head of the table. They all stand.*

Governor   Good morning, gentlemen. I've got some news for you. Appalling news. We're to be visited by an inspector.

A flash of lightning – half a second. The **Governor** *sits down.*

Judge   An inspector?

Charity Commissioner   An inspector?

Governor   A Government Inspector. With secret orders. Travelling incognito.

Judge   A Government Inspector!

Charity Commissioner   With secret orders!

Superintendent   Oh, God! He's incognito!

Governor   I had a feeling of impending bother. All last night I was dreaming about these weird rats. Two rats, giants both of 'em. Two giant black rats. And they came in. And they sniffed – everywhere, everything, everyone. They sniffed – and then they went away. Giants. And this morning, plonk on my mat, there's this letter from Andrey – you know him, don't you, Artemy? Anyway, here's what he says, 'My dear friend, godfather and benefactor . . .' (*He* *mumbles as he skips through the letter*.) 'So I rush to warn you that an official's arrived incognito with instructions to investigate the whole province, and especially our district. (*He raises his finger meaningfully*.) I've been tipped off by an unimpeachable source. I know you're human like the rest of us and we all have our little failings and you're not one to turn up your nose at the odd gift horse, wherever it drops from . . .' All in this together, aren't we? . . . 'So you'd best get cracking. He may manifest himself any moment. In fact, he may be in town already, incognito . . . Last Friday night I . . .' The rest is just family gossip . . . 'My sister Anna came to stay with her gloomy husband who weighs eighteen stone and plays Austrian rubbish on the fiddle' . . . etcetera and so on. And there you have it, gentlemen.

Judge   And it's unusual, decidedly . . . unusual. Yes, it's significant.

Superintendent   But why investigate our little town? Why should St Petersburg care what we get up to − I mean, how we conduct ourselves?

Governor   Why indeed? So far, thank God, they've been using their fine-tooth combs on other towns. But now the finger of fate is pointing − at us.

Judge   I think I perceive a subtle political motive. Russia is preparing to wage war, so an agent's been sent to root out any subversives.

Governor   Don't be daft. This isn't a frontier town. You could gallop from here for three years and never reach a foreign country. Thank God.

Judge   I'm not so sure. The authorities may be a long way off, but they've got eyes in the back of their heads. They've got dossiers on everyone. Everyone.

Governor   Maybe they have and maybe they haven't. True, at this very moment this Inspector may be fingering our records. Behind our backs. As far as my department goes − law and order and general amenities − I've already sprung into action. And you'd better all follow suit. (*He swings round on the* **Charity Commissioner**.) And that goes double for you, Artemy! This Inspector's bound to go over your hospital with a magnifying glass. And gimlet eyes. Get those patients of yours looking half-decent. They look like blacksmiths and stink like fishmongers.

Charity Commissioner I could have their nightcaps laundered.

Governor Right. And there should be some way of telling which patient is which and what they've got. Stick signs on the beds. In Latin or some foreign language – that's your line Doctor Gibner. Name of patient. When admitted. Name of disease. Likely to die or not . . . Hey, and stop the patients smoking such strong tobacco – dark brown spittle everywhere. And chuck out the ones who aren't that ill. Two to a bed looks bad, even if it does keep 'em warm. The Inspector'll think we've got a useless doctor.

Charity Commissioner Oh, as far as doctoring goes, don't worry about Doctor Gibner. He believes in nature cures – time is a great healer. We never use expensive drugs. Man's a simple creature: if he's going to die, he's going to die and vice versa. Anyway, Doctor Gibner doesn't waste his valuable time chattering to patients. They couldn't understand him if he did. Even for a German his Russian is worse than normal.

Doctor Gibner Das habe ich schon gesagt –

They all react blankly in a momentary freeze of incomprehension.

Governor And you, Amos, take a look at that courthouse of yours. The porters are keeping geese in the vestibule, the geese are having goslings and the public keep tripping over the goslings. I know it's patriotic to keep poultry, but there's a time and a place . . .

Judge Right. I'll have them shifted to the kitchen today. Would you care to drop round for dinner tonight?

Governor Another thing, that judge's office of yours. It's not exactly a shining example of the majesty of the law. Bearskins nailed up to dry on the oak panelling. Riding crops and saddles muddled up with the writs and summonses. I know you like hunting but can't you clear your equipment away till this Inspector's been and gone?

Judge Absolutely.

Governor And that clerk of yours ... Clever as they come, I grant you, but he smells like a distillery. I'd have mentioned it before, but it slipped my mind. Make him chew raw onions and garlic. Or maybe Doctor Gibner could give him something?

Doctor Gibner Sein Sie ruhig!

Judge Can't do much about that clerk. He says his nurse dropped him on his head when he was a baby and ever since then he's had this slight aroma of vodka.

Governor Just thought I'd mention it. Now ... 'We all have our little failings', as my friend Andrey puts it. I know you can't change human nature but ...

Judge Well, there's human nature and human nature.

Governor Yes. And there's bribes.

Judge Well, there's bribes and bribes, aren't there? Everyone knows I only accept borzoi puppies.

Governor Puppies or roubles – a bribe's a bribe.

Judge That's a bit strong. If someone feels like giving you a five hundred rouble fur coat, or, say, an Oriental shawl for your wife ...

Governor What do I care if you take borzoi puppies? But you're an unbeliever. You're never in church. At least I'm a good Christian, church every Sunday. But you ... When you start questioning the Creation, my hair stands on end, it really does.

Judge I've come to certain conclusions about the creation of the world by using my own brain.

Governor   There's such a thing as too much brain.
Anyway, your borzoi puppies won't save you if the
Inspector calls on your courthouse. Then it won't be
borzois, it'll be bloodhounds. (*To the* **Superintendent**.)
Right Luka, you're supposed to be Superintendent of
Schools, so it's up to you to do something about these
peculiar teachers of ours. I know they're a brainy bunch,
educated in all sorts of places, but they're odd as sabre-
toothed reindeers. There's that geography teacher. Three
years at the school and he still has to ask his way home.
And the maths master with the big fat face. Pulls horrible
faces all the time, like this. (*He makes a face.*) Of course it's
all right when he pulls faces at a pupil — it could be a new
teaching method, I wouldn't know — but what if he goes
like this (*He pulls a face.*) at the Inspector?

Superintendent   Can't do much with him. When we
had that royal visit he pulled a face like a walrus and
seemed to get stuck with it. And I got told off for
encouraging him to be a freethinker.

Governor   Try and make him stay home. Hide his pony.
And that history teacher. Knows his stuff, but he's mad as
a meat-axe. I heard him once. He was all right when he
was on about the Assyrians and the Babylonians, boring but
good. But when he came to Alexander the Great he went
berserk. You'd have thought there was a fire. He jumped
up on his desk and smashed his chair on the floor and
called for another chair and smashed it too and soon all
the boys were passing him their chairs . . . Well, of course
Alexander the Great was a distinguished monarch, but why
smash chairs? Municipal property.

Superintendent   He does get carried away. I gave him a
little lecture about it, but he just said 'You must do what
you imagine is your duty, Superintendent, but I would
gladly die on the battlefield of education.'

Governor   Yes, well, it's a queer world. Intellectuals are
always a bit touched. They either get lost or pull faces or

bust up the furniture.

Superintendent   God help anyone who goes in for teaching.

Governor   It'd be all right, all right . . . if he wasn't coming incognito. Any minute he may pop in and say 'Ah, there you all are. Who's the judge in this town?' 'Lyapkin-Tyapkin'. 'Come along with us, Lyapkin-Tyapkin. And who's in charge of the hospital?' 'Zemlyanika.' 'Zemlyanika, step this way.' It's really frightening.

The door opens and they all jump guiltily, except **Doctor Gibner**. *The* **Postmaster** *comes in.*

Postmaster   What's up? What's all this stuff about an inspector?

Governor   Haven't you heard?

Postmaster   Bobchinsky mentioned it. He just dropped by the post office.

Governor   What d'you make of it?

Postmaster   What do I make of it? I think it means war with Turkey.

Judge   Absolutely. Just what I said.

Postmaster   War with Turkey! All due to those bloody frogs.

Governor (*scornfully*)   War against Turkey? You're daft! War against us is more like it. We're going to be blown up, not the Turks. That's what this letter says.

Postmaster   Oh, that's different. There'll be no war with Turkey!

Governor   What does it all mean, Postmaster? How do you feel?

Postmaster   Bewildered mostly. How about you?

Governor   I face the future with confidence. But, I'm a bit bothered about the local merchants. They reckon I've been too demanding. Well, I may have encouraged them to make me little seasonal gifts, but I've been fair, for a Police Governor, I've been fair. (*Taking the* **Postmaster** *aside.*) Look, I fancy someone's put in a complaint about me. If not, why's this Petersburg snooper coming here? Listen, Ivan, this is for your own good as well as mine. Can't you take every letter that comes into your post office and well, just steam it open a little, you know, and skip through it. Then, if it's not denouncing anyone, you could seal it up and have it delivered.

Postmaster   You don't have to tell me. Why d'you think I keep the samovar going all day? I've been steaming for ages. Not just for security, mind. It's more that I like to know about current affairs and that. And I am partial to a good read, aren't you?

Governor   Anything in those letters about an inspector from St Petersburg?

Postmaster   Nothing about inspectors from Petersburg. But plenty about officials from Kostroma and Saratov. It's a shame you haven't read those letters. Unputdownable, some of them. Other day an army lieutenant wrote to his friend, describing a ball – very playful style, very vivid. 'I am, dear friend,' he wrote – to his friend – 'wallowing in the Elysian fields, surrounded by young ladies, with music playing and flags wagging.' Oh, he described it with great feeling. That's one I kept. Would you like a read of it?

Governor   Not now, Ivan. But look, if you find a letter with any moans or accusations, don't hesitate – file it.

Postmaster   My pleasure, your Excellency.

Judge   You know, they could really break you for this.

Postmaster   I wouldn't like that.

Governor   Nonsense. This isn't a public matter. Just a private arrangement.

Judge   Well remember, boiling water cools no chilblains. Actually, Anton, I was going to drop round with a little

dog for you. Sister to that dog you know, you know. Have
you heard that Cheptovich and Varchovinsky have started
suing each other? Suits me. Now I can shoot hares on
Cheptovich's land one day and Varchovinsky's land the
next.

Governor   I can't think about your hares. My head's full
of that incognito devil. What really gets me is that all we
can do is sit here. And wait. Wait for the door to burst
open and . . .

The door bursts open. Everyone, except the **Doctor**, *jumps. Enter,
panting,* **Bobchinsky** *and* **Dobchinsky**.

Bobchinsky   Amazing news!

Dobchinsky   Incredible goings-on!

All   What's up? What happened? What went on? (*Etc.*)

Dobchinsky   The mind boggles! I pop into the inn . . .

Bobchinsky   And I pop into the inn with Dobchinsky . . .

Dobchinsky   Let me tell them the story, Bobchinsky.

Bobchinsky   No, no, let me do it. You can't tell a story
like I tell a story.

Dobchinsky   You'll muddle it up. He muddles it up.
You'll leave out the best bits.

Bobchinsky   No. I'll put in the best bits. The worst bits
as well. Leave it to me, Dobchinsky.

Dobchinsky   But, Bobchinsky . . .

Bobchinsky   Oh, make him shut up!

Governor   For Christ's sake, let's have it. Spare my blood
pressure. Take a seat, Petr.

Dobchinsky *and* **Bobchinsky** *both try to sit in it.*

Governor   Now, what's all the fuss about?

Bobchinsky   Right. I'll start at the beginning and then
do the middle bit and finish up at the end. After you told

me about your letter, after you were so upset, yes, I went
and called on – let me finish, let me finish, Dobchinsky! I
know everything, everything, everything! So I slipped in to
see Korobkin, but he was out, so I nipped over to
Rastovsky's, but he wasn't home, so I whipped into the
post office to tell Ivan your news and coming out of there
who should I bump into but Dobchinsky?

Dobchinsky   Right by the hot pie stall.

Bobchinsky   Right by the hot pie stall. So I met
Dobchinsky and I said to him, I said, 'Have you heard
about the Governor's letter?' and he had, from your
housekeeper Avdotya down at the bottleshop, I don't know
what she was doing there . . .

Dobchinsky   Fetching a keg to put French brandy in.

Bobchinsky   Fetching a keg to put French brandy in –
let me finish, let me finish. So we toddled over to
Pochechuyev and on the way Dobchinsky said to me –
'Why don't we drift into the inn? My stomach's been
rumbling all morning.' My stomach – that's Dobchinsky's
stomach. 'They've got some fresh salmon in,' he said, 'We
could have a little snack,' he added. Right, so there we
were, ensconced in the inn, when a young man –

Dobchinsky   Very smart, but not in uniform

Bobchinsky   Very smart, but not in uniform, was pacing
round the room. He was thinking, thinking very deeply,
you could tell by his face. Yes, his face – it was a study –
a brainy face, very brainy. I had this funny feeling, so I
said to Dobchinsky 'Something's up, you know.' And he did
know, because he called Vlass, the landlord over. Vlass's
wife produced three weeks back – such a bright little chap!
He'll be like his father and run the bar some day. Well, we
had a word with Vlass and Dobchinsky put it to him, very
quietly 'Who's that young feller? Eh?' and Vlass said – let
me finish, let me finish – you'll get it all wrong and
anyway you lisp and whistle through that gap in your teeth.
So Vlass said 'That young man works for the government.

In Petersburg. Says he's off to Saratov. His name's Ivan Khlestakov and he's an odd customer. Been here two weeks, orders everything on tick and doesn't pay a kopeck.' And when he said that – I realised. And I said to Dobchinsky, I said 'Funny.'

Dobchinsky   No, Bobchinsky, I said it first. 'Funny,' I said.

All   Out with it. What was funny? You realised what?

Bobchinsky (*unruffled*)   Well, perhaps you said 'funny' first.

Bobchinsky }
Dobchinsky }   'Funny.'

Bobchinsky   And then we said 'Why's he sitting here if he's off to Saratov?' This is the one, all right.

Governor   What one?

Bobchinsky   The one you had that letter about. The Government Inspector.

Governor (*afraid*)   Impossible. God help us. It can't be.

Dobchinsky   He must be. Hangs around the town. Never pays cash. Who else could he be? And he's got someone with him.

Governor   Who's with him?

Dobchinsky   His manservant. Allegedly.

Governor   Allegedly . . .

Bobchinsky   But, this young Khlestakov . . . Oh. He's got eyes like gimlets. Nothing escapes him. He even noticed that we were eating salmon – because of Dobchinsky's stomach, you know. And he came over to our table. And he scrutinised our plates. I was petrified.

Governor   My God! Which room have they put him in?

Dobchinsky   Number five, under the stairs.

Bobchinsky The one where those Cossacks had that fight last year.

Governor Two weeks! He's been watching us for two weeks! Dear Christ! In the last two weeks the sergeant's widow's been flogged. And the prisoners haven't been fed. And the streets are full of ice and rubbish and beggars. The whole town's like a snowball full of turds. He'll destroy me!

Charity Commissioner Well . . . Shall we go and see him as a group?

Governor No, no! There are some ordeals that a man must face alone. I've had some rough times in the past, but I always survived. With God's help, of course. Perhaps . . . He's a young chap is he?

Dobchinsky About twenty-three, twenty-four at most.

Governor So much the better. Young men are easier to manipulate. The older they get, the tougher. Gentlemen, get your own affairs in order. I will go alone, or perhaps with Petr . . . Yes, we'll wander round to inspect the inn and make sure they treat their guests properly. Svistunov!

Enter **Svistunov**, *a police constable. (The name means whistler.)*

Svistunov Sir!

Governor Go and fetch the Police Inspector – no, I'll be needing you – go and fetch someone else to go and fetch the Police Inspector and then get yourself back here.

Exit **Svistunov**.

Charity Commissioner Let's be off. We've all got a few things to tidy up, I suppose.

Judge Not so bad for you. A few clean nightcaps for your patients, and you're sledding on greased runners.

Charity Commissioner Nightcaps are easy. But, the whole hospital reeks of cabbage soup.

Judge Well, I don't suppose he'll deign to poke his nose into my courthouse. Too bad if he does, of course. There's a cupboard marked 'Official Court Reports,' but it's full of trophies of the chase.

Charity Commissioner   Stuffed animals?

Judge   Well, yes . . .

The **Governor, Charity Commissioner, Schools Superintendent, Doctor Gibner** *and* **Postmaster** *start to go out but collide in the doorway with* **Constable Svistunov,** *who is returning. The* **Governor** *remains with* **Bobchinsky, Dobchinsky** *and* **Svistunov.**

Governor   Right. Where's Constable Prokhorov?

Svistunov   Laid up, sir. Unfit for duty.

Governor   What do you mean?

Svistunov   Staggered back this morning dead drunk, your Excellency.

Governor   My God! Get out in the street and − no, run upstairs and fetch my sword and my new hat.

Svistunov *goes into the house.*

Governor   Right, Dobchinsky, let's be off.

Bobchinsky   Me too, me too. Let me come too.

Governor   No, it'd begin to look like a deputation.

Bobchinsky   I wouldn't come in. I'd use the keyhole.

Svistunov *comes back with the sword and hat-box.*

Governor   Run along and get some women with snowshovels to scoop a road between here and the inn. Look − my grand sword of office, all tarnished. That wily old merchant, Abdulin − he was meant to polish it up. Probably forgot by mistake on purpose. Tradesmen! Expect they're getting a list of complaints about me written out for the Inspector at this very moment. Get them to clear that bloody snow. And you watch out, Constable Svistunov. I know you. Not above slipping a little cutlery into our jackboots, are we? And your little game with Chernyayev the draper, eh? He gives you two yards of cloth for a coat and you nick the whole roll. Watch out. Off you go!

Enter the **Police Inspector**.

Ah, there you are, Stepan. Where have you been hiding.

Police Inspector   At the gates, watching out for trouble.

Governor   The trouble's been inside the gates for the last two weeks. There's an inspector here from Petersburg. What have you done about it?

Police Inspector   Like you told me. I've sent Constable Pugovitzyn to form a street-sweeping party.

Governor   And where's Constable Derzhimorda?

Police Inspector   Out with the fire pumps clearing the beggars.

Governor   But Prokhorov's dead drunk. How did that happen?

Police Inspector   God knows. Yesterday there was a fight at the monastery. He went to sort it out and he came back pissed.

Governor   Listen. Stick that tall constable, Pugovitzin, on the bridge. He'll make a good impression, being so tall. Pull down that shabby old fence by the cobbler's and stick some poles in the ground. Give him the idea something's being planned. The more you pull down the more it'll look like enlightened civic government. Oh, God, I forgot! Everyone's been tipping rubbish over that fence for months. There's forty cartloads of stinking garbage there. What a horrible little town. Put up an elegant monument, a park, even a fence and they'll turn it into a dump. (*He sighs.*) Well, cover it with snow or something. And if this Inspector asks any of our constables 'Any complaints?' the right answer is 'No complaints at all, your Excellency.' And if anyone's got a complaint, I'll give 'em a complaint that's incurable. Oh, God. I have done those things that I ought

not to have done and I have left undone a few things that
I ought not to have done and I have left undone a few
things that I ought not to have done, too. (*He picks up the
hatbox.*) See me through this, O God, and I'll light you the
biggest candle the world has ever seen. Every merchant will
contribute half a ton of wax. Oh, my God. Let's go,
Dobchinsky. (*He puts on the hatbox instead of the hat.*)

Police Inspector That's the hatbox, your Excellency,
not the hat.

Governor (*throwing the box away*) To hell with hatboxes!
And if the Inspector asks why we haven't built that hospital
chapel, the one we raised funds for a few years back – say
we started building it, but it burnt itself down. I sent in a
report about it. Some sort of report. I think. And tell
Constable Derzhimorda to go easy with his fists. He seems
to imagine that justice consists of giving black eyes to
everyone. Let's go, Dobchinsky, and you, Bobchinsky. (*He
starts to leave but returns.*) And don't let the soldiers roam
around the streets half-naked. Underneath those great-coats
all they wear is their nightshirts. Don't ask me, for God's
sake, how I know.

They leave. Enter, running, **Anna Andreyevna** *and her daughter*
Marya.

Anna Where've they all got to? Where've they gone? (*She
opens the door to the hall.*) Anton! Anton! (*To* **Marya**.) It's all
your fault, Marya Antonovna, with your fussing around and
your 'whoops, there goes a hairpin' and your 'can't find my
scarf.' (*She runs to the window and calls.*) Anton! Where are
you off to? Has he come then? The Government Inspector
of course! Has he got a moustache? What sort of
moustache?

Governor (*off*) Later, my dear, later!

Anna Later! That's a revealing bit of news, isn't it? He's
gone! I'll not forget this, my girl. All your fault with your
'Mother, Mother, wait a minute. Help me fasten myself up,
Mother.' And so I waited a minute, and we know nothing.

Just because you heard the Postmaster clumping around downstairs, you started preening in front of the mirror. You think he's after you, but you should see the faces he makes when your back's turned.

Marya   Doesn't matter much, mother. We'll know all about everything in a couple of hours.

Anna   A couple of hours! Thank you very much. I am much obliged. And in a couple of months, perhaps, we'll hear even more. Hey, Dobchinsky! Come back here. (**Dobchinsky** *rushes back.*) What's he like? This inspector?

Dobchinsky   The Governor didn't say. He's in an awful hurry.

Dobchinsky *rushes off.*

Anna   Come back here at once! (**Dobchinsky** *rushes back.*) You should have grabbed him and stopped him and forced him to describe the man. Well, don't just stand there – listen! Run after that carriage! Hang on! Get after them, pick up a builder's ladder on the way, climb up it, look through the window and find out the lot!

Dobchinsky   Find out what?

Anna   What colour eyes he's got, black or otherwise. Complexion – red, white or blue – and a full description of his moustache. Then back here and report to me. Hurry, hurry, hurry!

Exit **Dobchinsky**.

Scene Two

A small room at the top of the inn, underneath the stairs. In it is a rickety bed, so placed that if you sit up suddenly you are certain to hit your head against the underside of the stairs. There is a chair set upon a card-table with one broken leg, and an expiring armchair.

On the walls are a few pictures – a long engraving of a battle scene with soldiers in three-cornered hats carrying huge drums and slender lances; besides that a huge, grimy oil painting of some flowers and fruit, half a water melon, a boar's head and a hanging, dead wild duck. There is a mirror which is broken so that you get four eyes instead of two.

Hanging from the ceiling is a chandelier in a holland covering, much too big for the room and covered in rust. A skylight is beside it.

On the floor, in one corner, is an abominable collection of objects, heaped up and mostly obscured by the dust of ages. Protruding from the pile is the shaft of a wooden spade, also a few shoes. More recent and thus recognisable additions to the pile include horse-collars, rope, a couple of sheepskins and a clock with four hands and a bent pendulum.

Osip *is lying on the bed.*

Osip   Hunger's a terrible thing, you know. My belly's rumbling like a bleeding volcano. And the way things are going, we'll never get home. More than two months since we left St Pete's. He's frittered and squandered for hundreds of miles and now all he can do is go to ground in the capital city of Nowhere. And he had plenty of cash, more than plenty, but everywhere we stayed he had to come on like a millionaire. (*He mimics* **Khlestakov**.) 'Hey, Osip, run along and book a room, the best in town. And order me a six- or seven-course meal. I can't digest cheap food.' Be different if he was somebody. But, he's just a jumped-up little clerk, hasn't jumped up very far and now he's fallen flat on his face. He meets a stranger – out comes a pack of cards – and he's done it again! That's the pattern, and I'm sick of it. Really, I'd do better to settle down in the country. There's not much excitement but there's not much trouble. You just find a woman, lie down by the stove and spend your life eating hot pies. Hot pies!

Ah, well, tell you the truth, you can't beat life in Petersburg. So long as you've got the cash, it's the height of civilisation. Theatre! Opera! Dancing dogs! They've got the lot. You saunter round the market stalls, everyone calls you 'honourable sir'. Cross on a ferry and you find you're rubbing shoulders with a government official. Or an army officer wearing a golden medal will tell you anecdotes of life under canvas or explain the meaning of every star in the sky. Or you may find yourself kissing the hand of an officer's wife, or a pretty young parlour maid may smile at you and serve you with salted cod. (*He smiles and shakes his head.*) And there's never a cross word, never a dirty look in Petersburg. And if your feet are getting frayed, jump in a cab and sit back like a lord, and if you've got no money, that's all right, every house has a side gate, you nip through and you've done the vanishing trick.

But this is different. Six- or seven-course meals one week. Fasting unto bursting the next – like now. It's all his bloody fault. His dad sends him money. But does he save it? No. He's out on the razzle: cab rides, theatre tickets, rings on his fingers and bells on his – and next week he sends you down to Uncle's to pop his new tail-coat. Worth a hundred and fifty, but he'll pawn it to raise twenty. And why? Because he's skiving off work, that's why. Because he should be in the office totting up government accounts. But he's swanning down the boulevard, down a back-street and into a card game with the devil, a couple of vultures and an octopus. Ah, if only your old dad could see you now. You may be a civil servant, but he'd civil servant your bum for you till you couldn't . . . but, knowing you, you'd play cards standing up.

Just now the landlord told me he wouldn't give me any more food till the bill's paid. (*Sighing.*) Oh God, if you would only grant me some cabbage soup. I think I could eat the whole of Russia. With Japan for afters.

There is a sudden earthquake in the bed. **Khlestakov** *has been down in the bed, asleep. He sits up indignantly. He wears an overcoat.*

Khlestakov   Get out of my bed.

Osip   Thought it was our bed.

Khlestakov   It's my shift.

Osip   I'm only taking up the edge.

Khlestakov   It's not your shift. You're absorbing the

warmth of the bed. You're dishevelling the sheets.

Osip (*standing*)   I can take a hint. I'll walk up and down. Lovely walking up and down. Warms the blood.

Khlestakov   Look in the bag. Maybe there's some tobacco left.

Osip (*looking in the bag*)   You smoked the last of it four days ago. Before you tried smoking the carpet.

Khlestakov *leaps out of bed. He paces up and down, then confronts* **Osip**.

Khlestakov (*loudly*)   Hey! Listen to me, Osip.

Osip   What is it?

Khlestakov (*still loud, but not so determined*)   Osip, I want you to go there.

Osip   Go where?

Khlestakov (*wheedling*)   To the kitchen. Tell them that the gentleman in room five requires his lunch.

Osip   No. I'm not that keen on going.

Khlestakov   But you're my servant. You're responsible for my welfare.

Osip   Look, even if I do go, it won't do any good. Landlord told me: no more lunches.

Khlestakov   That must be illegal. I'm a traveller.

Osip   Well, you haven't been travelling for the past two weeks. Anyway, the landlord says he'll tell the Police Governor that you won't pay up. You and your master, he said to me, are a couple of swindlers and your master's a right villain.

Khlestakov   You're enjoying this, aren't you?

Osip   He said to me, 'You're a pair of crooks. You move in here, live it up, run up a bill you can't pay and then think you can sit tight and call for the bloody menu. I'm off to see the Governor, he said to me, and you'll end up in a hostelry in Siberia on black bread and dirty water.

Khlestakov   That's enough of that. You go and teach him manners, Osip.

Osip   I could ask him to come and have a natter with you.

Khlestakov   No, I don't really hit it off with him for some reason. You go.

Osip   Anything you say.

Khlestakov   The hell with it! Fetch the landlord! (**Osip** *goes out.* **Khlestakov** *takes off his overcoat to reveal rather fashionable clothes.*) Hunger's a terrible thing, you know. I thought maybe I could walk off my hunger, but it's worse than ever. You can't run away from your stomach, as the old people say. If I hadn't gone on the booze in Penza, I'd have had the cash to get home. It was that infantry captain finished me off. Must've been a conjurer before he joined up. Talk about a shifty shuffler! Fifteen minutes, and he cleaned me out. Wish I could've got my own back, but I didn't have the capital. What a nasty little town this is! Bloody shopkeepers won't put an onion on the slate. The mean-mindedness of the provinces!

Khlestakov *walks up and down whistling. Enter* **Osip** *and the* **Waiter** *in tow. The* **Waiter** *has a red face and a permanent, forgiving smile.*

Waiter   Lovely day, sir. Landlord sent me.

Khlestakov   Lovely day if you like skeletons. How's business?

Waiter   Thriving, thriving, thank the Lord.

Khlestakov   Plenty of customers?

Waiter   Very nice crowd, sir, yes, very nice.

Khlestakov   Waiter. Waiter – listen. I've had no meal today. Let's have a bite of dinner, eh? I've got an important after-dinner engagement. So, I've got to have some dinner first, haven't I?

Waiter The landlord says 'No more dinners for number five.' He's going to talk to the Governor about you.

Khlestakov Talk to the Governor? What for? Look, waiter, I need food! Take a good look at me. Emaciation can go no further. I need a good, big hot meal. And that's nothing to grin about.

Waiter I'm sorry, sir. I smile because I'm happy. I'm happy because I'm saved. Because Jesus died for my sins. But the landlord says, 'No more meals till number five pays his bill.'

Khlestakov Explain to him. Appeal to him. Money is not the issue. Or does he want to find my bones gathering dust upon his carpet?

Waiter Very well, sir. God bless you.

Exit the **Waiter**. *Also* **Osip**.

Khlestakov God bless – Oh, if I don't get a meal. It's terrible. Genuine hunger pangs! I suppose I could sell my trousers. Or eat them? No, it's better to starve and arrive home wearing a suit cut in Petersburg. What a pity they wouldn't let me rent a carriage without a deposit. It would have been wonderful to arrive home in a troika, to go thundering over the landscape to visit one of those grand houses where the gentry live, with Osip wearing my gilded livery. The driveway crowded with barouches, their lanterns gleaming, a couple of gendarmes posted beside the great white doors, a babel of postillions' cries as footmen with flaring torches in their hands leap forward to greet the slim and distinguished figure of the mysterious stranger. At the upper windows, the feminine excitement is unbounded. 'Who can he be? An ambassador? A prince?' And then the voice of the major-domo booms out through the great hall; 'Ivan from Petersburg.' The whole family pull on their tiaras and hurry down to greet me. And there I stand in the light of the chandeliers. Poised. Suave. An inclination of the head, the slightest of smiles as I raise the hand of a young princess to my lips. 'May I be permitted . . .' Ooh! It's a terrible thing to starve!

Osip *comes in, followed by the* **Waiter** *carrying a tray of food.*

Khlestakov   Well?

Osip   Dinner is served.

Khlestakov *pulls the chair off the table and sits on it.*

Khlestakov   Dinner! Dinner!

Waiter   This is your last lunch. The landlord said so.

Khlestakov   Landlord! May he rot in . . .

Waiter   Sir!

Khlestakov   What's for dinner?

Waiter   Turnip soup and cold veal.

Khlestakov   Only a two-course dinner?

Waiter   That's all, sir.

Khlestakov   Ridiculous! I'll cancel my order! Go and tell him I need three courses at least! Four!

Waiter   The landlord says two's more than you deserve, sir.

Khlestakov   All right, why is there no gravy on the cold veal?

Waiter   Because there is no gravy.

Khlestakov   You deny the existence of gravy? But this morning, passing the kitchen, I saw a great big bowl of gravy under a cloud of gravy-steam and I took a sniff and . . . and then I took a short cut through the dining room and there were two little fellers feeding their faces with salmon. Do you claim that there is no such thing as salmon?

Waiter   Well, sir, yes and no.

Khlestakov   Are there no chops? No caviar? No mountain ashberry tart soaked in corn brandy?

Waiter   They would be for special customers.

Khlestakov   You're an evil man.

Waiter   I am sir, but Jesus loves me.

Khlestakov   Jesus. Look, what's so special about these special customers?

Waiter   They pay for their food, sir.

Khlestakov   It's wicked. I'll ignore you. (*He ladles out soup and eats.*) Turnip soup? It's washing-up soup! It doesn't taste of anything except earth. Waiter! This soup is not to my liking. There are lumps in it.

Waiter   I'll take it away, sir. The landlord says if you don't like it, you can lump it.

Khlestakov (*protecting his soup from being taken away*)   Don't touch it, you soup-thief! This may be how you treat your ordinary customers, but I'm not ordinary. (*He drinks more soup.*) Good grief! I'm the only man in the world who could swallow this stuff. There's a little yellow beak in it. And some newspaper. (*He tries to read it.*) 'Cotton yarn, jute yarn, alpaca, mohair and woollen flannel were in demand, but . . .' You may finish the soup, Osip. (*He cuts the veal.*) Waiter, this substance is not veal.

Waiter (*interested*)   What is it, then, sir?

Khlestakov   Embalmed blubber? It should be a criminal offence. Wonder what the special customers are eating? If you try to chew it, it sort of sucks your teeth out of your gums. Isn't there anything else?

Waiter   No, sir.

Khlestakov   It's highway robbery! No gravy. No mountain ashberry tart. It's an insult to the human stomach!

The **Waiter** *and* **Osip** *clear away the food and leave.*

(*Clutching his stomach.*) The void! I ate just enough to make me really hungry. If I had the money I'd send out to the market to buy a humble little roll.

Osip *comes back.*

Osip The Police Governor's turned up. He's with the landlord asking about the gentlemen in number five.

Khlestakov (*scared*) What? That bloody landlord's called in the law already? What if he sticks me in jail? Well, if they feed me like a gentleman I might . . . No, no. I won't go. The whole town'd talk. And they think of me as rather . . . distinguished. Especially that pretty redhead in the baker's shop. No, I'll not be arrested. What does he think I am – a shopkeeper? A plumber? (*He screws up his courage and straightens up.*) I'll tell him to his face. 'What the hell do you think you're doing? How dare you?'

The **Governor** *comes in, sees* **Khlestakov** *and stops. Both men are scared stiff. They stare at each other in silence, without moving. The* **Governor** *recovers first, and stands to attention.*

Governor May I present my compliments to you?

Dobchinsky *creeps in.*

Khlestakov And mine to you, too.

Governor I hope I'm not butting in . . .

Khlestakov Not in the slightest.

Governor As governor of this town it's my privilege to ensure that everything goes smoothly for important people.

Khlestakov (*stammering at first, but loud towards the end of his speech*) But what can I do? I haven't done anything. I'm going to pay, of course I'm going to pay.

Bobchinsky *peeps round the door.*

Khlestakov You can blame it on the landlord. His veal's like India rubber. The soup's like mud. Thin mud! The tea tastes of smoked mackerel. The whole inn's a national disgrace! Why should I be forced to . . .

Governor (*intimidated*)   Please forgive me. It really isn't my fault. Our town's famous for good meat. I can't think where the landlord buys such rubbish. But, since you're unhappy here, perhaps I can offer you more appropriate accommodation.

Khlestakov   Never. I'm not leaving. Appropriate accommodation! You mean the jail, don't you? I know my rights. How dare you? I'll . . . I'm employed by the government in Petersburg. I, I, I . . .

Governor (*aside*)   Oh, Lord! He's furious. He knows everything. Those damned shopkeepers must have spilled the beans.

Khlestakov (*getting bolder*)   Bring in the Cossacks, but I won't go! The only place I'll go is to the ministry! To the minister! (*He bangs his fist on the table.*) What do you think of that?

Governor (*very scared*)   Sir. Please. I must throw myself on your mercy. Please don't ruin my career. I have a wife. Little children. Don't destroy me!

Khlestakov   And because you've got a wife and children, I have to go to jail? Wonderful!

Bobchinsky *looks in, then draws back, terrified.*

Khlestakov   No, thank you very much! You'll not take me there.

Governor (*trembling*)   I'm not a worldly man, your Excellency. God knows it was just my inexperience and unworldliness! And my pathetic salary. Work it out for yourself – my official salary wouldn't even keep us in tea and sugar. So, if I have accepted the odd bribe, it was only an innocent little one – to buy a couple of pork chops or some dresses for my daughter. As for the story that I had the sergeant's widow flogged – it's a filthy lie! My enemies invent these stories. Yes, I've got enemies. And I've reason to believe they're plotting to assassinate me.

Khlestakov   Well, that's your problem. (*Thinking.*) Why

are you telling me all this, about your enemies and the
sergeant's widow? A sergeant's widow is one thing, but
you'd better not try flogging me. I wouldn't try it! I'll pay
my bill and move on when my money comes through, but
till it does I'm staying here. To be honest, I've got no cash
whatsoever.

Governor (*aside*)   Oh, he's crafty! Hinting, hinting. Well, a
shout's as good as a whisper to a deaf Kulak, as the old
folk say. So long as it was a shout. Better make sure.
(*Aloud.*) If you are at all financially embarrassed, you'll find
me at your service. Part of my job, you understand.
Helping a visitor to enjoy his stay in our little community.

Khlestakov   A loan, that's very civil! Then I can pay
that landlord straight away. Two hundred roubles would
take care of it, or even less.

Governor (*handing over the money*)   Two hundred exactly.
Don't bother to count it, please.

Khlestakov (*accepting the money*)   Very kind of you. I'll pay
you back as soon as I get home to my place in the country
. . . Unexpected circumstances . . . You're a real gentleman,
I can tell.

Governor (*aside*)   Thank God! He took it! We'll pull
through! And I managed to slip him four hundred roubles
instead of two hundred.

Khlestakov   Hey, Osip!

Osip *enters.*

Khlestakov   Fetch that waiter!

Exit **Osip**. **Khlestakov** *turns to the* **Governor** *and*
Dobchinsky.

But why are you standing up? Please take a seat. (*To*
Dobchinsky.) Sit yourself down.

Governor   It doesn't matter, we've been sitting down a
lot.

Khlestakov Do me a favour, sir, and sit down. Now I can see how straightforward and generous you are. I must admit I thought you'd come to ... (*To* **Dobchinsky**.) Sit down!

The **Governor** *and* **Dobchinsky** *sit down on the bed, which sags dangerously.* **Bobchinsky** *peeps through a skylight and listens.*

Governor (*aside*) I'd better take the initiative. He obviously wants to preserve his incognito. All right, we'll do some double-talking too and pretend we don't know who he is. (*Aloud.*) I came round here on business you see, with Petr, one of our leading landowners, to find out how the inn treats visitors to our town. I'm not one of your governors who doesn't bother with things like that. I don't have to do it, of course, but I like to do it, and it's my duty as a Christian to see that every traveller who comes this way is treated like St Christopher treated Our Lord.

Dobchinsky *works this out, doing a little seated mime of St Christopher taking Jesus for a ride on his shoulders.*

Governor And, like St Christopher, I have my reward – the honour of meeting you, sir.

Khlestakov It's rewarding for me, too. If it wasn't for you I'd have been stuck here for ages. Didn't know how I was going to pay my bill!

Governor (*aside*) A likely story! He's on government expenses. (*Aloud.*) May I ask where you're travelling to?

Khlestakov On my way to the family estate in Saratov Province.

Governor (*aside*) Saratov! And he says it with a straight face! You've got to keep on your toes with this one! (*Aloud.*) How delightful! They can talk about potholes and delays with horses, but the scenery's amusing. And I assume you're travelling for pleasure?

Khlestakov No, my father told me to come home. He's angry because I haven't been promoted yet. He thinks that as soon as you arrive in St Petersburg they pin the Order

of Vladimir on you. He ought to try a week in my office.
It's very boring.

Governor (*aside*) What a wonderful smokescreen! Nice
touch, the old father! (*Aloud.*) Do you expect to be staying
with us long?

Khlestakov I'm not sure yet. You see my dad is a stupid
man, stupid. Thick as a tree stump. I'm going to tell him,
'Babble on,' I shall say, 'Babble on, but I tell you, father, I
cannot live except in St Pete's. Why should I throw away
my life among peasants? My heart starves for enlightenment
and culture and all that!'

Governor (*aside*) What a performance! Cover story after
cover story and they all match! But he's a scrawny, sneaky-
looking chap. I could crack him like a flea. I'd better put
in a word for myself. (*Aloud.*) You're right, there's not much
for a man to do in these outlandish places. I mean, look at
me. Can't sleep for worrying about municipal problems,
wearing myself to a frazzle for the national benefit, leaving
no stone unturned for the general good. A slave to duty,
you might say, but the Order of Vladimir doesn't grow on
trees, not round these parts. Oh no, I'm hidden under a
bushel. (*Looking around the room.*) Your room seems rather
chilly.

Khlestakov It's a filthy, fungussy slum of a room. The
only good thing I'll say for it is that the damp patches on
the mattress have frozen over so you can have fun
watching the bedbugs skating.

Governor It's not good enough! A distinguished guest
having to put up with fungus and bugs . . . I didn't know
there were any bugs in this part of town. Black bugs, are
they?

Khlestakov Yes. And spotty yellow ones, too.

Governor And it's pretty dark in here, too.

Khlestakov Cold and dark. The landlord charges for
every candle. So if I want to read a little, or if I'm inspired

and feel like writing – well, I can't. Because it's dark, dark, dark.

Governor   I wonder if I could ask you ... but, I couldn't. It's not my place.

Khlestakov   Ask me what?

Governor   No! No! I could hardly hope ...

Khlestakov   What is it? Ask me.

Governor   Well, there's a rather tasteful room in my house ... full of light ... very dry ... But, it would be too great an honour! Please don't be angry, I'm a simple man. I just happen to believe in hospitality.

Khlestakov   Don't worry about it. It would give me the greatest pleasure. How much nicer to reside in a private house, than to be trapped in this flea circus.

Governor   I'm overwhelmed – and my wife will be delighted. Even as a child I enjoyed entertaining guests. And such a distinguished guest! But don't think I say that to butter you up! I'm just a blunt countryman. When a thought comes into my head, I just say it. Like the wolf in the butter churn.

Khlestakov   Me, too. I'm like that. I hate hypocrites. You're a straightforward chap and a warm host, and I like you for it. I don't ask much from people, I don't expect much, frankly, but there are two things I like to see in a man – understanding and consideration for others.

Enter **Osip** *and the* **Waiter**.

Waiter (*respectfully*)   Is there anything I can bring you, sir?

Khlestakov   The bill, my man!

Waiter   I gave you the latest one this morning, sir.

Khlestakov   I can't be expected to keep track of all your daft bills. What's the damage?

Waiter   Well, the first day you had beef, sir, the second day you had salmon and after that you had credit.

Khlestakov   He's crazy as a bee-keeper. Give us the total.

Governor   Please don't trouble yourself with that. The landlord can wait. (*To the* **Waiter**.) Get out. I'll settle up later.

Khlestakov   That's right, later, waiter.

Khlestakov *puts away his money.* **Bobchinsky** *peeps in through the skylight, leaning a little further this time.*

Waiter (*leaving*)   God bless you both, sirs.

Governor   Perhaps you'd like to inspect some of our institutions while you're here?

Khlestakov   What've you got?

Governor   The usual ... It's just a town ... show you round.

Khlestakov   A tour of the town? That sounds fine.

Governor   You'd like to study our teaching methods? We could visit the school.

Khlestakov   Excellent.

Governor   Then there's crime prevention. We would have an informal chat with the Inspector at the police station.

Khlestakov (*suspicious*)   The police station? I'm really more interested in your charity work.

Governor   Of course. And your assistant?

Osip   I'll come too. I'm very interested in charity work.

Governor (*to* **Dobchinsky**)   Listen, you deliver a couple of notes for me, quick as you can: one to Zemlyanika at the hospital and one to my wife. (*To* **Khlestakov**.) D'you mind if I scribble a note to my wife? Tell her to get the room ready for you.

Khlestakov   Of course. I've got ink, but no paper. Here, use this bill. (*He produces a bill from his pocket.*)

Governor   That'll do nicely. (*To himself while writing.*) We'll see how things go after a bumper of port and a good dinner. There's a local custom of improving Madeira with vodka. It'll knock out an elephant.

The **Governor** *finishes the note and gives it to* **Dobchinsky**, *but at the same moment* **Bobchinsky** *falls through the skylight and clings on to the chandelier, which gradually sags down on to the bed, which finally collapses. General exclamations.* **Bobchinsky** *gets up.*

Khlestakov   Are you all right, there?

Bobchinsky   Quite all right, quite all right. Please don't worry. Just a slight bang on the nose, you know. I'll run over to Doctor Gibner. He has a wonderful nose plaster. You just plop it on your nose and – abracadabra – you feel fit to get married.

Governor (*to* **Khlestakov**)   Take no notice. Shall we go?

Osip *picks up* **Khlestakov**'*s trunk, which he has been packing.*

Governor   After you.

Khlestakov *goes out. The* **Governor** *turns on* **Bobchinsky**.

Governor   If you want to practise falling out of windows, try the bell tower!

The **Governor** *leaves, followed by* **Osip** *and* **Bobchinsky**.

Blackout.

Scene Three

The drawing room of the **Governor**'*s house. A warm, plush room, somewhat overdecorated with oil paintings, screens, busts, etc. The high bourgeois style of the 1830s. The furniture should seem slightly too small for the people who sit on it, except for one vast, comfortable leather armchair which is usually reserved for the* **Governor**. *But in this act, at least, it is only occupied by* **Khlestakov** *so that he can*

*make himself super-comfortable, even curling up in it like a cat, while
the others have to perch and shift. [For descriptions of interiors and
furnishings, Gogol's* Dead Souls *is recommended.] A clock. And a
sideboard with bottles. There is a double french window, or period
equivalent, at the near centre upstage, but this is covered, through most
of Acts One and Two, by velvet curtains. There should be thick rugs,
a steaming samovar, a fire blazing — total contrast to the chilly little
hutch in the inn scene. There is another window, at which* **Marya**
and **Anna** *are standing.*

Anna You see, we've been waiting a whole hour, and all
because of your fussing. You were perfectly decently
dressed, but you weren't satisfied, were you? You had to
keep dawdling and primping. Nobody's coming! They're
not coming on purpose to annoy me. It looks like the
whole world's dead.

Marya Honestly Mother, we'll know all about it in two
ticks!

Anna (*disgusted*) Two ticks!

Marya Dobchinsky must be back soon. Ooh, look,
Mama, someone's coming. Look, right down at the end of
the street.

Anna Where? You're over-imaginative! Oh! There is
somebody. Who is it? Little fat feller. Who is it? You know
I'm short-sighted.

Marya It's Dobchinsky, Mama.

Anna Dobchinsky, indeed! Rubbish! Dobchinsky can't
move that fast, I mean quickly. (*She waves her handkerchief.*)
Hey, you! get a move on.

Marya Honestly, Mama, it's Dobchinsky.

Anna You're just saying that to fluster me. 'Course it's
not Dobchinsky.

Marya There you are! It is Dobchinsky. Told you so.

Anna All right, it's Dobchinsky. What are you arguing
about? (*She shouts out of the window.*) Hurry up then! Stop

loitering. Where are they? You what? No, tell me from
where you are, I can hear you. What? Very stern is he?
And how's my husband? (*She moves back from the window.*)
He's hopeless, won't tell me anything till he comes in.

Enter **Dobchinsky** *sprinting and panting.*

Come on, out with it! Aren't you ashamed of yourself? I
counted on you, Dobchinsky I counted on you. And you
just dashed away with the rest of the pack! Like the snake
in the haystack. And I'm stuck here for hours without
knowing what's up. I was godmother to your Vanichka and
Lizanka and this is all the thanks I get.

Dobchinsky   Just a minute. I'm puffed out. How are
you, (*Gulps.*) Marya?

Marya   Good afternoon, Petr.

Anna   Good afternoon, good night, good morning and
what's up?

Dobchinsky   Anton sent you a note.

Anna   But who's the stranger? A general?

Dobchinsky   Not exactly a general, but as good as. Very
educated. Very good manners.

Anna   So it's the one my husband had the letter about.

Dobchinsky   Precisely. And it was me that found him.
Me and Bobchinsky.

Anna   Tell us about it, then.

Dobchinsky   Well, everything's all right, thank God. So
far. At first he was a little brusque with Anton. Yes. He
was very vexed and he said the inn was terrible and he
wouldn't go to jail because of that. But, when he found out
it wasn't the Govenor's fault and got to know him better,
he calmed down, and then, thank God, eveything went like
clockwork. They've gone for a tour of the town. I think the
Governor reckoned at first that there'd been a confidential
complaint about him. And I wasn't so happy myself.

Anna   Why should you be worried? You're not a government servant.

Dobchinsky   Important people make me nervous.

Anna   Never mind about that. What's he like? Old or young?

Dobchinsky   Young! A young man! About twenty-three. But he talks like an old man. 'There's an old head with a young face,' I said to myself. And he talks with natural dignity. (*Making dignified gestures as he demonstrates.*) 'Let this be done, and that. I will visit this place, and this place. How nice! How very nice! I like to read sometimes,' he said, 'and I write too, when the inspiration comes on. What a shame this room is so dark.'

Anna   Is he dark? Or fair?

Dobchinsky   Dark, very dark. And eyes like, what d'ye call 'em, gimlets. Dark gimlets.

Anna   The note!

Dobchinsky *gives it to her. She reads.*

'Dear Anna, well it looked pretty black for us, but I trusted in God for two pickled cucumbers separately and half a portion of caviar one rouble twenty-five kopecks.' (*She stops.*) I don't quite understand. What's cucumbers and caviar got to do with anything?

Dobchinsky   He wrote it in a hurry. On some sort of bill.

Anna   I see. 'But I trusted in God and it seems that it'll all work out. Get a room ready quick for our distinguished guest – the one with the yellow wallpaper – and build up all the fires. Don't worry about dinner. We'll be eating with Artemy at the hospital, but order plenty of wine. Tell Abdulin to send up a crate of his best burgundy or I'll turn his cellar upside down. I kiss your hand and remain yours Anton Skvoznik-Dmuchanovsky.' My God! We'd better get on with it! Hey, who's there? Mishka!

Dobchinsky (*runs and shouts through the door*)   Mishka!
Mishka! Mishka!

Enter **Mishka**.

Anna   Listen, scuttle down to Abdulin's . . . Wait, I'll give
you a little note. (*She sits at the table and writes while speaking.*)
Give this note to Sidor the coachman, tell him to drive
down to Abdulin's and pick up the burgundy. And brandy.
And you go and tidy up the yellow room. He'll need a
washstand and all that.

Dobchinsky   I'm off then, Anna. I'd better see him
inspecting the hospital.

Anna   Off you go then! I'm not stopping you. Right then,
Marya, what're we going to wear? He's a Petersburg
sophisticate – so we don't want to look like folk dancers.
You'd better wear your pale blue dress with the little
flounces.

Marya   Oh, no, Mother. Flounces are out. And the
Judge's wife wears pale blue and so does that Zemlyanika
girl. Much better if I wore my one with the flowers of
spring.

Anna   Flowers of spring indeed! You're trying to spite me.
Just because I want to wear my sallow ivory. My sallow
ivory shows off my figure so nicely.

Marya   Oh, Mother! Your sallow ivory makes you look
vulgar.

Anna   Vulgar?

Marya   Yes. You need dark googly eyes to get away with
that neckline.

Anna   What do you mean? I've got dark eyes. Course I
have. Very dark. And googly. Of course they're dark. I
always draw the Queen of Clubs when I'm having my
fortune told.

Marya   Queen of Hearts, more often.

Anna   Rubbish! Absolute rubbish! I never get the Queen of Hearts.

Marya   Well, I'm still torn between my flowers of spring and my flame-coloured velvet.

Anna   How about the frothy pink and white one . . .

Marya   Well, perhaps . . .

Anna   That makes you look like a plate of meringues?

Anna *and* **Marya** *exchange glares and leave, unbuttoning for their next change.* **Mishka** *begins to clear up.* **Osip** *comes in with a suitcase.*

Osip   Where can I dump this lot, mate?

Mishka   Through that door, up the stairs, down the corridor, second on your left.

Osip   Hang on. Let's have a breather. Bust the icicles off my fingers.

Mishka   Is the General coming soon?

Osip   What general?

Mishka   Your master, of course.

Osip   He's not a general.

Mishka   No?

Osip   Not exactly.

Mishka   Well is he higher or lower than a general?

Osip   Oh, higher. You can't get much higher.

Mishka   I thought so. That's why everyone here's running round like loonies.

Osip   Listen, lad. I can see you've got your head screwed on. How about a snack?

Mishka   Dinner isn't ready yet. But it won't be a snack when it comes. When your boss eats, you'll get the same as him. And it'll be a proper feast.

Osip   All right, but I need some now. What've you got handy?

Mishka   Cabbage soup, porridge, meat pie.

Osip   All right, I'll have . . . cabbage soup, porridge and meat pie. Whatever you've got. Give us a hand with the clobber.

Mishka *and* **Osip** *carry the case out.* **Constables** *open the door. Enter* **Khlestakov**, *followed by the* **Governor**, *the* **Charity Commissioner**, *the* **Schools Superintendent**, **Dobchinsky** *and* **Bobchinsky** *with a plaster on his nose. The* **Governor** *points to a piece of paper on the floor.* **Dobchinsky** *and* **Bobchinsky** *compete to pick it up. Everyone is trying to put on a big show — except* **Khlestakov**.

Khlestakov   That was a nice hospital. And a nice courthouse. And the school was . . . (*He considers.*) . . . nice. It's not every town that gives you a grand tour. Some towns I've been through they don't show me anything.

Governor   Ah. But in some towns, maybe, the governor's got nothing much to be proud of, eh? But in this town everyone pulls together and we've got one big ambition: to show the world that we're up-to-date, efficient, honest folk!

Khlestakov   That was a marvellous lunch. Big portions. Plenty to drink.

The **Governor** *signs to* **Dobchinsky** *and* **Bobchinsky**, *who rush to fetch* **Khlestakov** *a drink. From now on he has two glasses which are constantly being replenished from bottles on the sideboard.*

D'you throw a banquet like that every day?

Governor   Oh no, we're very economical. But for a special guest . . .

Khlestakov   I love good food. But then, what is life all about?

They all ponder this furiously.

I believe we are put on this earth ... to have a good time. That fish we had, what was its name?

Charity Commissioner   Hake, your Excellency. Baked hake.

Khlestakov   Baked hake. Truly delicious. Hey, what was that big place we had lunch at? Looked like a hospital. (*He laughs.*)

Charity Commissioner   It *was* the hospital.

Khlestakov   Of course it was, there were many beds, many beds. And not many patients.

Charity Commissioner   We've got about ten left, no more. Since I took over, with Doctor Gibner and his German methods, they've been recovering like flies. It's not so much that we're medical wizards. I put it down to honesty, hygiene and strict discipline in the wards.

Governor   But of course you don't have a heavy case-load, do you, Artemy? I mean, the people round here aren't all that prone to diseases, are they? But when you look at the picture as a whole, like the governor has to – then you've got problems, real problems. So many things to be looked after, nothing must be neglected – sanitation, law and order, education, repair and maintenance, snow clearance. Running a town is a complex operation. But, thank God, this one runs pretty smoothly. I know some Mayors are only out for what they can get, but you know, every night when I blow out the light beside my bed at four in the morning, maybe, I say to myself 'Oh God, all I ask for in my work is just a little recognition. Perhaps I'll be granted official honours and perhaps I won't, but at least I'll have the satisfaction of a job well done! The town's developing, the streets are clean, the patients are all getting better and there are no drunks on our streets. What more could a governor ask? But I'm not after a decoration, mind! Very nice for the chosen few, I'm sure, but what's the Order of Vladimir compared with the satisfaction of a life well spent. Dust! Dust and ashes! That's all.'

Charity Commissioner   You say all that to yourself every night?

Governor   Well, most nights.

Khlestakov   Dust and ashes. Very true. I'm fond of philosophy myself. Sometimes I do it in prose. Sometimes I do it in a song.

Bobchinsky (*to* **Dobchinsky**)   There you are, Petr, he's an astonishing man. You can see that he's been to university and studied something . . .

Khlestakov   But what do you do for a bit of fun round here? Don't you ever get down to a game of cards? (*He reaches in his pocket for a pack of cards but he doesn't produce one.*)

Governor (*aside*)   Oh yes, testing us out to see if we're gamblers. (*Aloud.*) God forbid, we never gamble here. Actually, I can honestly say I have never ever held a playing card in my hand in the entire course of my life. Just looking at cards makes me feel queer. Once I had to entertain the orphans and they made me build them a house of cards. You know, I had to go out and be sick. I'll never understand how some people fritter their time away with cards.

Superintendent (*aside*)   Only three days ago he won a hundred roubles off me.

Khlestakov   Oh, now look. If you've been losing at cards, don't get sour. Sometimes it works if you treble your stake. Win it back. A good game of cards is like . . . (*All lean forward for wisdom.*) a battle. In miniature. With less blood. No blood. You know.

Enter **Anna** *and* **Marya**, *who have changed, changed utterly.*

Governor   May I introduce my family? My wife and daughter.

Khlestakov (*rising and bowing*)   I am extremely delighted to meet the both of you.

Anna   It's a great honour for us to meet such an

important person.

Khlestakov (*taking on airs*)   Not at all, not at all. My honour is greater. For me. In meeting you.

Anna   What a graceful compliment, sir. But please, sit down.

Khlestakov   But I feel very happy standing up beside you! But if you would like me to, I will sit down. I would feel very happy sitting down. Beside you.

Khlestakov *and* **Anna** *sit down.*

Anna   Travelling must be very trying compared with life in Petersburg.

Khlestakov   Yes, it's awful. You're accustomed, comprenez-vous, to high society and suddenly you find yourself on the road: grubby inns, crooked landlords, stupid people of all kinds. But sometimes (*Making up to* **Anna**.) you do meet a warm sympathetic, real human being – like you – and that makes up for everything.

Anna   Still, it must be almost degrading for such an important . . .

Khlestakov   Not at the moment. I don't feel degraded at all. Everything is wonderful.

Anna   You're just being polite. We don't deserve it.

Khlestakov   You'll never get – anything in the world that's good enough for you.

Anna   I'm just a simple countrywoman.

Khlestakov   The country! Ah! The country, with its little streams and little flowers and little sheep and stuff. But you can't compare it with Petersburg. Ah. Petersburg. Perhaps you think I'm just a copying clerk? Oh no, I'm on very good terms with the head of my department. Many's the time he pops into my office, slaps me on the back and says, 'Come on, Ivan Alexandrovich, feeding time on Nevsky Prospekt.' So I tell my department what to be

getting on with and the copying clerk, little rat-like fellow
he is, begins scratching away with his pen – tr, tr. They
wanted to promote me, but I've got enough responsibility
as it is. And then the porter runs after me on the staircase
with a brush, 'Mr Khlestakov, please let me polish your
boots.' But why are you all standing up?

All   Out of respect for your rank. We want to hear you
better. We like standing up. We're quite happy.

Khlestakov   Gentlemen, please be seated.

They all sit.

I don't stand on ceremony. No. I try to be inconspicuous.
Don't like to be noticed. Ah, but it's not possible. As soon
as I step into the street the cry goes up, 'Look there goes
the famous Khlestakov!' Once I was even taken for the
Commander-in-Chief. The Imperial Guard turned out and
presented arms to me. Of course, at the time I wondered
why, but a colonel who's an old friend of mine told me
afterwards, 'You know, old man, they were absolutely
convinced it was the C-in-C.'

Anna   Good heavens!

Khlestakov   Well, they know me everywhere. Some of
my best friends are pretty actresses. I've written a few bits
and pieces for the stage, you see. Another thing about
Petersburg, I keep bumping into famous writers I know.
Alexander Pushkin and I are like that. (*He indicates with his
fingers.*) Whenever I see him in the street I say, 'How are
you doing, Pushkin?' And he gives me a friendly punch,
you know, and he says, 'I'm muddling through, Ivan,
muddling through!' (*Suddenly pugnacious.*) You can say what
you like, but he's a good sort, Pushkin.

Anna   You're a writer too? How nice! Do you write for
magazines, too?

Khlestakov   Oh yes, magazines too! And I've done some
plays: *The Marriage of Figaro, Robert le Diable, Norma* – I can't
remember them all. It's not my fault. Theatre managers

won't leave me alone. 'Write us another play, old boy, we need another hit.' So I think to myself, 'Why not?' And I go scribble, scribble, scribble, and before dawn – another masterpiece! And everyone's astounded – except me. Seems to me the most natural thing in the world, I've got a mind like a jumping frog, as they say in St Pete's. All the Baron Brambeus stuff, and *Pride and Prejudice* and the *Moscow Daily Telegraph* – samples of my work.

Anna   So you are the great Baron Brambeus?

Khlestakov   Of course. And I rewrite verses for all the best poets, correct their rhymes and so on. They club together and pay me 40,000 a year for that.

Anna   It wouldn't surprise me if you wrote *Childe Harold*, you sly thing.

Khlestakov   You found out my secret!

Marya   But Mama, it says on my copy that it was written by Lord Byron.

Anna   You think your mother's illiterate, don't you?

Khlestakov   Oh, that's Byron's *Childe Harold*. My *Childe Harold* is rather more – ambitious?

Anna   Well, it must've been yours I read about. I read a wonderful review of it.

Khlestakov   Did go down rather well. But I'm the first to admit it. I live for art. Everyone in Petersburg knows my house. The police point it out to foreigners. 'That – the house – of Khles-ta-kov.' If you're ever up in Petersburg, drop in on me, please. I hold rather exceptional parties.

Anna   I can just imagine.

Khlestakov   You cannot. The buffet, for example. On the sideboard, for instance, a . . . a seven-hundred-rouble watermelon. (*Gasps from the others.*) And a tureen of special soup, shipped straight from Paris. One lifts the lid, one bathes one's nostrils in the perfumed steam. Pushkin couldn't describe it. If I'm not giving a party, I'm out at some elegant ball. There's a little group of us like to play whist together in a corner: the Foreign Minister, the French Ambassador, British Ambassador, German Ambassador and me. (*He realises that he's counted wrong, on his fingers.*) That's five, so we chuck out the German. Ah, whist! So exhausting! So home I go and I dash up the stairs to the fourth floor and say to the cook, 'Hang up my coat, Mavrusha!' (*He stops and laughs.*) – that'd make a good opening for a story wouldn't it, but of course I live on the ground floor, and the second floor, third floor, fourth floor and so on – a whole great house and my marble staircase alone is worth ... And I wish you could see my hall, in the morning, before I even wake up – there are counts and princes swarming and buzzing around like bees round a hive and all you can hear is zh ... zh ... zh. Even sometimes a Government Minister, buzzing like the rest ... zh ... zh.

The **Governor** *and others stand up, nervously.* **Khlestakov** *is drunk and highly excited, becoming more and more cheerful but not slurring his words.*

Even my letters come addressed 'Your Excellency.' Yes, once I was put in charge of the whole department. It was very weird. Our boss had gone off. Vanished. Nobody knew where. And then of course there were the same old arguments – who's going to take over? Some of the generals wanted the job and they tried it, one after another. But they hadn't got it, they hadn't got it – here. (*He taps his head.*) Say what you like about the men at the top, but oh, when you get up there ... it's not so simple. No! They found out. Yes. And so they asked me. They sent urgent messages every minute. The streets were thronging with messengers. Can you imagine a street? Right. Now imagine it filled with thirty-five thousand messengers. And I come out on my balcony and I say, 'What can I do for you, my friends?' And thirty-five thousand messengers shout with a single voice, 'Your Excellency, Ivan Khlestakov, go and take charge of the Department!' It was a bit embarrassing, I was still in my dressing-gown – which is embroidered

with golden foxes – so I went and changed and when I was
ready I found ministers of state and princes and elders of
the church kneeling in silent prayer at the foot of my
marble staircase which is worth ... And I looked at them
and I said, 'Gentlemen, what do I want with power?' And
they set up such a piteous whimpering sound, ah, it would
crack your heart. And I thought – I thought of the Czar,
and how he'd feel if I refused. So I said, 'Get up off your
knees – I accept. But gentlemen, but, I – I – I have eyes
in my head. So you'd better watch out and if any of you
try to ...' And you know I marched through that
department like some great elephant, like an enormous
elephant. And everything and everyone in that building
trembled, trembled, trembled.

They all are now trembling like mad. **Khlestakov** *is very worked
up, his speech more violent, but still clear.*

No, I don't fool about! I flogged them with my tongue! I
even put the fear of God into the state council. That's it!
That's how I am! Nobody stops me! I told them, 'I know
everything! I see everything! I know you! And you! And
you!' I call round at the palace every day! Tomorrow I'm
going to be a field marshal. (*Staggering during the last sentences
he now slips but is caught and respectfully supported by officials.*)

Governor (*shaking with fright, he can hardly speak*)   Your ...
your ... you ...

Khlestakov (*abruptly*)   What's up?

Governor   Your ... your llency, excellency. Would you
like to lie down? Your room is all prepared. You'll find
everything you need.

Khlestakov (*standing, swaying slightly*)   Lie down? Never!

Nobody contradicts him.

Of course. Lying down is good. Hey, gentlemen!

They all tense themselves for denunciation.

That was a good meal. Very good! I am extremely happy!

Khlestakov *totters to the door towards his room; suddenly he veers round and opens a cupboard door instead, mistaking it for his door. A mass of old papers and documents falls all over him. All crowd round and help him to his feet. The* **Governor** *gently guides him to the right door. At the door,* **Khlestakov** *turns round.*

Baked hake! Baked hake!

Khlestakov *turns and goes, supported by the* **Governor**. *The audience is given time to see the expression of those left on stage.*

End of Act One.

Act Two

Scene One

*The meeting room in the **Governor**'s house, the morning after.*

Governor Constables!

*Enter **Derzhimorda** and **Svistunov**, noisily.*

Shhhh! Enter two clumsy bears. They perform clog dance. Can't you tiptoe in those boots? Where the hell have you been?

Derzhimorda As I was proceeding to carry out my orders –

Governor (*clasping his hand over the constable's mouth*) Shhhh! And now, the leading bear with sing an aria. (*He imitates him.*) 'As I was proceeding . . .' It sounds like someone throwing barrels of molasses off a cart. Now listen. You two go and stand on the front steps and don't move. Whatever happens. Nobody gets in here today. Especially those merchants. And anyone with a petition, no, anyone who even looks like he wants to hand in a petition – exit head first down the steps, right? (*He demonstrates a mighty kick.*) Like this. Understand? (*He suddenly realises he's talking too loudly.*) Shh! Quietly! Right, get going.

Derzhimorda and **Svistunov** *tiptoe off to guard the front door.*

Governor (*Alone.*) The world's getting stranger and stranger. Important people used to look important, but these days . . . He's thin, no, skinny – he could be anybody. He didn't give much away at the inn, talked a lot of red herrings. But last night he gave away a bit more than he should. You can see he's new to the game.

Anna and **Marya** *come in, all dressed up.*

Anna Anton! That dressing-gown! You look like a wandering hermit! What'll he think?

Governor　He's still sleeping it off! But keep your voice down, my darling! My brain's all addled. I feel like a man in a condemned cell. My neck's all tense. Couldn't sleep all night for worry.

Anna　I wasn't frightened of him at all. Seemed like a nicely brought up, educated gentleman to me. I didn't give a thought to his position.

Marya　I think he's lovely.

Anna　He's got that Petersburg air. He's so suave and sophisticated. I took to him straight off! And he kept aiming meaningful glances at me.

Marya　Oh, Mama! Those meaningful glances were aimed at me.

Anna　You're not very worldly, are you Marya? Why'd he bother with you? Any more remarks like that and it's up to your room.

Governor　Women! That one word sums you up. Wonder how much of what he said was true. Maybe it's all true. When a man's sozzled, it all pours out. He probably threw in a few little white lies, everyone does that. He plays whist with the Foreign Secretary and goes to the palace every day! But he can certainly put it over. Very convincing.

Osip *comes in from the direction of* **Khlestakov***'s room, shutting the door very quietly behind him.*

Anna　Good morning.

Governor　Is your master still asleep?

Osip　He's stretching a little bit.

Anna　Listen, er, what's your name?

Osip　Osip, madam.

Governor (*to* **Anna** *and* **Marya**)　That'll do, that'll do. (*To* **Osip**.) All right, my friend, have they fed you all right?

Osip   Very good meal, thanks a lot.

Anna   I suppose your master's visited by lots of counts and princes?

Osip (*aside*)   If I get this one right I should win an even better meal. (*Aloud.*) Oh yes, crowds of them.

Marya   Oh, Osip, he's so good looking!

Anna   I'd be interested to know just how he . . .

Governor   That's enough! I can't get a word in. Now, Osip . . .

Anna   What's your master's rank?

Osip   The usual, what you'd expect.

Governor   What a stupid question! Listen, my friend, is your master very strict? You know? Does he enjoy finding fault with people? Or is he easy-going?

Osip   He just likes things to run smoothly. He likes everything – just right.

Anna   What does he look like in uniform?

Governor   Oh, my God! This is a matter of life and death. Now, Osip, what sort of things does your master watch out for? When he's travelling around? What does he like best of all?

Osip   That depends, doesn't it? Mostly he likes to be looked after properly.

Anna   Listen Osip, what colour eyes does your master like best?

Marya   Oh, Osip, he's got such a perky little nose.

Governor   I'll give you a perky little nose! Now, Osip, what were you going to say?

Osip   Well, he does like being looked after. I do my best for him. And he does very well by me. Pretty often we've stayed somewhere and afterwards he puts it to me: 'They look after you all right, Osip?' 'No sir, they did not sir,' I say sometimes, 'Treated me like a pig, they did.' 'Right,' he says to me, 'That town goes on my black list. Remind me when we get back to Petersburg, Osip.' And I think to myself, 'God bless him.'

Governor (*after a brief pause*)   Osip, you're the salt of the earth, as the fishermen say. You know something, I like your face. You must need the odd hot drink to warm you up on the road these days . . . Here's a few roubles for tea.

Osip (*taking the money*)   God bless you sir, I'll drink your health with that.

Anna   Come here, Osip, I've something for you too!

Marya   Sweet Osip, will you give your master a kiss from me?

There is coughing outside the door leading to **Khlestakov***'s room.*

Governor   Shhhh. (*He whispers.*) Let's have total quiet.

Anna   Come on, Marya, I've got a couple of things to say to you about our guest. We're going to have a little talk.

Anna *and* **Marya** *go out.*

Governor   Those little talks! Enough to make the wallpaper blush. Right, Osip, you're a good chap, here's a little more for a meal or two on the road to Saratov.

Osip   You're a good man, sir.

Governor   I wish I was, Osip, I wish I was.

Osip *leaves and, on tiptoe, enter the* **Schools Superintendent***, the* **Judge***, the* **Charity Commissioner***, the* **Postmaster***,* **Dobchinsky** *and* **Bobchinsky***, all in full dress uniform. This whole scene is played in whispers.*

Governor   Well, gentlemen, you're up bright and early aren't you?

Charity Commissioner   We came to pay our respects . . . to him.

Governor (*to* **Dobchinsky** *and* **Bobchinsky**)   And you, Petr?

Dobchinsky   Oh, I've got to see him about something terribly urgent!

The **Judge** *and* **Governor** *exchange knowing glances and coughs.*

Governor   Has that school of yours pulled itself together, Luka Lukich?

Superintendent   Oh, I give up. (*He shrugs hopelessly.*) What can you do with people?

Governor   Well, my friends, I'll be with you in a minute. I must get dressed and take care of a few little items.

The **Governor** *exits anxiously as a further bout of coughing, worse, is heard from behind* **Khlestakov**'*s door.*

Judge   For God's sake gentlemen, arrange yourselves in a semi-circle! And smarten up! He's a regular visitor at the palace! Try and look more military. Petr – that end. And Petr, over here. (*There is some confusion in which* **Dobchinsky** *and* **Bobchinsky** *change places, on tiptoe.*)

Charity Commissioner   I don't know about you, but I reckon we ought to take some action.

Judge   Action?

Charity Commissioner   You know what I mean? Um . . .

Judge   Not? (*He makes a bribery gesture.*)

Charity Commissioner   I thought we ought.

Judge   No, much too dangerous. It'd be like tipping an international statesman. We could raise a subscription and pay it into some fund for a memorial or something – that's more like it!

Postmaster   Or we could say, 'Oh look, this money just came in the post – and it's got no address on it!'

Charity Commissioner   Watch out he doesn't put you

in the post with no address on you. You can't do things like that in a law abiding country. Now, why are we all here in a mob? We should see him one by one. Then, whatever goes on, there's no witnesses. That's how things get done in a law abiding country. You go first, Ammos.

Judge   Much better if you went first. I mean, you gave that feast for him at your hospital.

Charity Commissioner   Perhaps Luka should go first – representing education and youth and all that.

Superintendent   I don't . . . no. I couldn't. Much too nervous. It's the way I was brought up. Just put me in a room with someone one rank above me and I shake and stutter and . . . really, gentlemen, leave me out.

Charity Commissioner   No, you ought to go first, Ammos. You're a modern Cicero.

Judge   That's putting it a bit – well, I suppose I can make a speech, if the subject's right. I mean I can talk about dogs till the cows come home . . .

All   Come on, Judge! You're much too modest! You're the one. You don't just talk about dogs. You made a good speech about the Tower of Babel. Oh Ammos!

Judge   That's enough, gentlemen!

There are steps and more coughing from behind **Khlestakov**'s *door. Everyone rushes for the other door to see who can get out first. There is a crush in the door.*

Bobchinsky   Oh Petr, Petr, you're standing on my foot.

Dobchinsky   I'm sorry! I thought it was my foot.

There are more exclamations as all push through and vanish.
Khlestakov *emerges, rubbing his eyes. He is hungover and his hair is sticking up.*

Khlestakov   Oh, what a wonderful kip! Nothing like a feather bed. A good snore and a good sweat, as my old mother used to say. That wine was amazing. My head's like a beehive. I think I can have a very nice time here. I do like warm-hearted people. And it's all the better because they're not putting themselves out because they want something. They just like me for what I am. Hey, that daughter's not bad as they go and they do go you know, and the mother – ready for anything. This is the life!

Khlestakov *collapses into the* **Governor***'s chair. Enter the* **Judge**.

Judge (*drawing himself up and putting his hand on his sword*)   Actually, we met yesterday, but you won't remember me. I'm the district judge. Ammos Fyodorovich Lyapkin-Tyapkin.

Khlestakov   Sit you down. So you're the Judge. Good money is it?

Judge   It's more the honour, you know. I've been awarded the Order of Vladimir, Fourth Class, with the approval of my superiors. (*Aside.*) I've never held so many roubles in my hand before.

Khlestakov   I like the Order of Vladimir. But I've got no time for the bloody Order of St Anna, Third Class.

Judge   No. Oh, no. (*Aside.*) What do I do now?

Khlestakov   What's in your hand?

Judge (*panicking and dropping notes on the floor*)   Absolutely nothing.

Khlestakov   Nothing? That looks like money on the floor. (*He picks it up.*) It is – money.

Judge   No, it's not. Is it? Oh, good. Money, that's lucky. Finders keepers you know.

Khlestakov   I'll tell you what. Can you let me have a loan of these? You know how it is when you're travelling around, bit short of the ready. Pay you back when I get to my parents' place. By post.

Judge   Not at all, don't give it a thought. Only too glad to help. Absolutely. Work as a team, that's my motto. Very good of you to spare me your time, your Excellency. Have you any orders?

Khlestakov   What kind of orders?

Judge   About how I should run the court for instance.

Khlestakov   Not at this particular moment, thanks.

Judge (*aside as he bows out*)   What a relief.

Exit the **Judge**.

Khlestakov   Nicest judge I ever met!

Enter the **Postmaster** *in full dress coat, hand on sword.*

Postmaster   May I present myself – Postmaster Shpekin.

Khlestakov   Come in. I like good company. Sit down. Always lived round here, have you?

Postmaster   Absolutely correct, sir.

Khlestakov   It's a nice little town. Not so many people of course, but so what? It's not the capital, is it?

Postmaster   Sir?

Khlestakov   Not the capital, is it?

Postmaster   Yes, that's right. It's not.

Khlestakov   The great thing about the capital is that there are so many fashionable people and so few provincials, don't you agree?

Postmaster   That's what I think. (*Aside.*) Well, he's not toffee-nosed. He listens to other people's opinions.

Khlestakov   But let's admit it, it's possible to live happily, even in a small town?

Postmaster   I admit it.

Khlestakov   I mean, what does one need as one trudges through life, what does one really need? One needs respect, and genuine friendship and not much more, does one?

Postmaster (*valiantly trying to keep in step*)   One does not.

Khlestakov   I'm very very glad we're of the same
opinion. Of course, lots of people think I'm peculiar, but
that's just because of my character. (*Aside.*) I'll tap this one
for a loan, too. (*Aloud.*) You know a funny thing happened
to me while I was travelling – I completely ran out of cash.

The **Postmaster** *laughs, then stops.*

Could you lend me three hundred roubles?

Postmaster   That would make me a happy man. (*He
hands over the money.*)

Khlestakov   Thanks a lot. The thing is, when I'm
travelling, I do hate having to go without. And why should
I go without?

Postmaster   Precisely. I wouldn't go without. If I were to
travel, that is. (*He gets up and stands erect, hand on sword.*) I
don't dare to trouble you any more. Will there be any
instructions about the running of the post office?

Khlestakov   There will not.

The **Postmaster** *bows and leaves.* **Khlestakov** *lights a cigar.*

The Postmaster's a good sort, too. Very obliging. I like
these people.

The **Schools Superintendent** *is almost pushed through the
door as we hear a remark from the far side of the door, 'What are
you scared about?'*

Superintendent (*standing to attention, terrified, hand on
sword*)   Can I introduce myself – Schools Superintendent
Khlopov.

Khlestakov   Fine. Take a seat. Have a cigar.

Superintendent   I can't remember if I smoke.

Khlestakov   Go on, take it, it's not bad. Of course, I
have my own cigars rolled for me in Petersburg. Yes, with
a portrait of me on the band. Have a light. (*He holds out a*

candle.)

The **Superintendent** *tries to light the cigar, but trembles too much.*

Try lighting the other end.

The **Superintendent** *drops the cigar, spits and gives up.*

Superintendent   Damn it! I haven't felt like this since I was a schoolboy, waiting to be beaten.

Khlestakov   You don't strike me as a cigar man. Cigars are my favourite vice. Next to women, of course. Hey, what about you? What kind of women get you going? Brunettes or blondes?

The **Superintendent** *is lost in cosmic embarrassment.*

Come on, which is it, brunettes or blondes?

Superintendent   I'm not really sure, I mean . . .

Khlestakov   Come on! I like to know these things. Oh, you're a sly operator. But I can tell. It's the dark, curly ones for you, isn't it? Look, you're blushing. I knew I was right.

Superintendent   I don't really know, your Excellency, I mean . . . (*Aside.*) Oh God, he's a mind-reader. (*Aloud.*) I'm a bit overawed by you.

Khlestakov   Don't worry. Lots of people have that problem with me, it's my gimlet eyes. Women are transfixed by my gaze. You see?

Khlestakov *does an intense stare.*

Superintendent   I can see they would be.

Khlestakov (*after a pause*)   A funny thing happened to me on my way to this place. All my money ran out. Could you lend me, say, three hundred roubles?

Superintendent (*aside*)   What if I haven't got it? (*Aloud.*) I've got it. I've got it! (*Hands over the notes, trembling.*)

Khlestakov   Many thanks.

Superintendent   Well, I'll be running along.

Khlestakov   Goodbye.

Superintendent (*almost running out, aside*)   Thank God!
With any luck he won't inspect the school!

Enter the **Charity Commissioner**, *hand on sword.*

Charity Commissioner   May I have the honour?
Charity Commissioner, Zemlyanika.

Khlestakov   Sit down, very nice to meet you.

Charity Commissioner   Oh. I had the honour of
conducting you round the hospital yesterday.

Khlestakov   That's it. The hospital. That was a classic
lunch, classic!

Charity Commissioner   We do as best we can for our
visitors, sir.

Khlestakov   If there's one thing I like, it's a really hefty
meal. Hey! You look smaller than you did yesterday.

Charity Commissioner   That's quite possible. (*Pause.*)
All I can say is that I don't stint myself when it comes to
working for the good of the community. (*He moves his chair
up to speak confidentially.*) I wish I could say the same for
everyone. The local Postmaster, for instance. Do you know
what's in the post office pigeon holes?

Khlestakov   No.

Charity Commissioner   Pigeons ... The Judge, who
was here just now, he's more interested in pursuing hares
than justice –

Khlestakov   That's a nice phrase ...

Charity Commissioner   He keeps dogs and his
behaviour – it's my patriotic duty to tell you this even
though he's my friend and we're related by marriage – his
private life's a scandal. There's a landowner around town,

Dobchinsky, you may have noticed him. Well, whenever Dobchinsky leaves his house, the Judge adjourns his court and whizzes round to call on Mrs Dobchinsky. And that's not just gossip. You just look at the children, sir. Not one of them looks like Dobchinsky. But all of them, even the little girl, are the spitting image of the Judge. If you forget the moustache, of course.

Khlestakov   I didn't think he had it in him.

Charity Commissioner   As for the Schools Superintendent . . . I don't know how he was chosen, but he's like an anarchist in sheep's clothing, putting political ideas into young minds. I can write all this out for you if it'd be convenient.

Khlestakov   Good idea. That'll be handy. I like a good read. What's your name again? I forgot.

Charity Commissioner   Zemlyanika.

Khlestakov   Oh, yes, Zemlyanika. And do you have any children yourself?

Charity Commissioner   Of course! Five. Two already grown up.

Khlestakov   And what are their names?

Charity Commissioner   Nicholas, Ivan, Peter, Catherine and Perpetua.

Khlestakov   Very patriotic.

Charity Commissioner   I won't trouble you any more. I know you're a very busy man.

Khlestakov (*showing him out*)   Don't mention it. That was a good conversation. Come and see me again. Oh, by the way what's your name again, I keep forgetting.

Charity Commissioner   Artemy Zemlyanika.

Khlestakov   That's right. Well a funny thing happened to me – I ran out of money on the way here. Got any cash you can lend me, say, four hundred roubles?

Charity Commissioner   Of course.

Khlestakov   Very good of you, old man.

Exit the **Charity Commissioner**. *Simultaneously,*
Bobchinsky *and* **Dobchinsky** *burst in.*

Bobchinsky   May I introduce myself? I am a small
landowner – Petr Bobchinsky.

Dobchinsky   May I introduce myself? I am a small
landowner – Petr Dobchinsky.

Khlestakov   I've seen you before. You'd just fallen
through a skylight. How's the hooter?

Bobchinsky   Oh, please don't worry about me, sir. It's
mending nicely, thank God.

Khlestakov   That's lucky, I'm very pleased. (*Abruptly.*) Got
any cash on you?

Bobchinsky   Cash? Er what . . . why?

Khlestakov   I could do with a loan of a thousand
roubles.

Bobchinsky   Oh, dear. I haven't got that much. You
don't happen to have a thousand on you, do you
Dobchinsky?

Dobchinsky   Sorry. (*To* **Khlestakov**.) You see I keep all
my money in a savings bank.

Khlestakov   Well, if you haven't got a thousand, a
hundred would help.

Bobchinsky (*fumbling in his pockets*)   Haven't you got a
hundred, Dobchinsky? I've only got forty in notes.

Dobchinsky (*looking in his wallet and counting*)   Twenty-five
roubles, twelve kopecks.

Bobchinsky   Keep looking. Your right hand pocket's got
a hole in it, so the money's probably fallen into the lining.

Dobchinsky   No luck.

Khlestakov　Well, if all you've got is sixty-five roubles . . . never mind. (*He takes the notes.*)

Dobchinsky　Do I dare ask you about a rather embarrassing problem, sir?

Khlestakov　Of course. About women, is it?

Dobchinsky　Not exactly, sir. Our eldest boy, well, he was born before we got married . . .

Khlestakov　Yes?

Dobchinsky (*embarrassed*)　But only in a manner of speaking. It was as if we were married and now we are. So what I'd like, if you follow me, is that he should be my own legitimate son, and have the same name as myself – Dobchinsky.

Khlestakov　All right, let him take the name, that's fine.

Dobchinsky　Oh, I wouldn't have bothered you, but it's such a pity because he's so talented. We're sure he'll do well. He can say lots of poems by heart. And if you just give him a penknife and a lump of wood he'll carve you a little carriage, just like magic. That's right, isn't it Bobchinsky?

Bobchinsky　Yes, the boy's very bright.

Khlestakov　Good. Good. I'll see about it. I'll talk about it and I hope – something will be done. Yes. (*To* **Bobchinsky**.) You've got something to tell me?

Bobchinsky　Just one little request, sir.

Khlestakov　Let's have it.

Bobchinsky　I'd just ask you sir, when you go back to St Petersburgh, and you see all those senators and admirals and nobles . . . could you say to them, 'You know Your Grace or Your Majesty as the case may be, there's a man who lives in such and such a town and his name is Petr Bobchinsky.' Just that 'And his name is Petr Bobchinsky.'

Khlestakov　I will almost certainly do that.

Dobchinsky   Please forgive us for taking up your time.

Bobchinsky   Yes, please forgive us for taking up your time.

Khlestakov   Not at all. My pleasure.

Dobchinsky *and* **Bobchinsky** *leave.*

Khlestakov   Takes a lot of jockeys to run a one-horse town. And they've mistaken me for some big noise in the government. What a gang of loonies! I must have been in good form yesterday. Oh, I'll have to write to Tryapitchkin about this. He does those funny articles, he could make a really hilarious one of this lot. Osip!

Osip *looks round the door.*

Khlestakov   Ink and paper!

Osip   Give us a minute.

Osip *vanishes.*

Khlestakov   Hey! It's great when that Tryapitchkin gets his knife into somebody! He'd cut up his granny for a good gossip item. Or for cash down. He's very fond of money. But they're a generous bunch, the people who run this town. Let's see how much I've collected. Three hundred from the Judge, three hundred from the Postmaster, six, seven, eight hundred ... what a filthy note ... eight hundred, nine hundred ... well over a thousand. I'd like to meet that infantry captain now! I'd teach him how to play cards.

Osip *comes in and gives him paper and ink.*

Khlestakov   There you are, stupid. You see how they treat me. They know a gentleman when they see one, even if you don't. (*He writes.*)

Osip   Very nice, too. But you know something, Ivan?

Khlestakov   What?

Osip   I think we ought to get moving. It's about time.

Khlestakov   Nonsense. What for?

Osip   Because it's vanishing time. Don't want to outstay our welcome. You don't know what'll happen if we hang about here. Anyone might turn up. Honestly, Ivan. The horses they've got, they're beauties. We'd be over the horizon in no time.

Khlestakov   But I'm having a good time. Let's hang on till tomorrow.

Osip   Tomorrow? Better hop it today. All right, they're buttering us up now, but that's because they think you're someone else, you know that? And your father'll go mad if we don't get back soon. We could be off in half an hour. They'd give us the best horses.

Khlestakov (*still writing*)   Oh, all right. But take this letter to the post office. Tryapitchkin will die laughing. And, while you're at it, order me some horses, and a good carriage.

Osip   I'll send the letter with one of the servants, sir. I'd better start your packing. Save time.

Khlestakov   All right.

Osip (*speaking to someone off-stage*)   Hey! I've got a letter for the post office, tell the Postmaster to take care of the money, and tell him to send round the very best troika for my master. The government's paying . . . And tell him to get cracking, my master's in a nasty mood. Hang on, the letter's not finished yet.

Khlestakov (*writing*)   I wonder where he lives now. He likes to move from flat to flat . . . saves rent. I'll take a chance that he's still living on Post Office Street (*He rolls up the letter and addresses it.*)

Derzhimorda (*off*)   Who are you pushing, fuzz-face? Nobody's going in, nobody!

Khlestakov (*giving* **Osip** *the letter*)   Here, take it.

Merchants' Voices (*off*)   We want to come in. We're

entitled to see him. Business. It's about business.

Derzhimorda (*off*)   Get out of here! He can't see you.
He's asleep.

The noise gets worse.

Khlestakov   What's up, Osip? Have a look.

Osip (*at the door*)   It's a gang of merchants.

Khlestakov (*going towards the door*)   What's the matter, my
good people?

Merchants (*through the crack in the door*)   We appeal to you,
your excellency. Something's got to be done. Read our
petitions.

Petitions are crammed through the door.

Khlestakov   Get them organised, Osip.

Osip *sorts out the merchants, allowing three into the room.*
Khlestakov *picks up a petition and reads.*

'To his most Noble Reverence, the Master of Finance, from
the merchant Abdulin.' Master of Finance – there's no such
rank!

The **Merchants** *bow to* **Khlestakov** *and deposit their goods in
front of him.*

Was there something you wanted?

Merchants *appear at the sides of the room; they thrust their
petitions through the 'walls'.*

Merchants (*from the sides*)   Petitions! Petitions!

Khlestakov   One at a time, please.

1st Merchant   We need your help.

2nd Merchant   We're honest merchants.

3rd Merchant   We're being ruined.

Khlestakov (*'shocked'*)   Oh no! Who's responsible?

A silence. **Merchants** *look at each other.*

1st Merchant   It's the Governor, sir. He's the worst in the history of the town.

2nd Merchant   He billets soldiers on us.

3rd Merchant   They eat us out of house and home.

1st Merchant   He pulls our beards.

2nd Merchant   Shouts down our throats.

3rd Merchant   He stamps into our shops and grabs whatever he sees.

1st Merchant   'Good morning. That's a nice piece of cloth you've got there. Bring it round to my house.'

2nd Merchant   For his wife and daughter's dresses.

Khlestakov   Sounds like a real crook.

3rd Merchant   He doesn't just like the good stuff.

1st Merchant   Old dried-up prunes – seven years in the barrel.

2nd Merchant   He gulps them down in handfuls.

1st Merchant   Even my shop assistant wouldn't eat 'em.

3rd Merchant   But if you try and say anything to him he'll billet a whole regiment on you.

2nd Merchant   Or he'll shut your shop.

1st Merchant   'I won't have you tortured,' he'll say, 'because that would be against the law. But from now on you'll get nothing but salted herrings.'

Khlestakov   People get sent to Siberia for that sort of thing.

1st Merchant   We don't mind where you send him as long as it's a long way.

2nd Merchant   A long long way.

3rd Merchant   A long long long long long long way
away.

Khlestakov   That's a long way.

1st Merchant   Please accept these sugar loaves.

2nd Merchant   And this wine.

Khlestakov (*sternly*)   No! No bribes! Bribes are bad.

Merchants   Yes, bribes are bad.

Khlestakov   But loans are good.

Merchants   Loans are good.

1st Merchant (*whispering to colleagues*)   Three hundred
roubles each.

Merchants (*muttering*)   Three hundred . . .

Merchants *hold out money.*

3rd Merchant (*offering money on a silver tray*)   A loan, sir.
And please accept the loan of a tray as well.

1st Merchant   And the sugar

Khlestakov   I hate sugar!

Merchants   A loan, sir, a loan.

They thrust money on **Khlestakov**, *bigger and bigger notes. It
starts to snow money from above.* **Khlestakov** *restrains himself
from snatching the money.*

Khlestakov   Osip! Collect my loans!

Merchants   Please help us, sir.

Khlestakov (*shouts*)   I'LL DO MY BEST!!

The **Merchants** *vanish. The door bursts open. The*
Locksmith's Wife *and* **Sergeant's Widow** *kneel at*
Khlestakov's *feet.*

(*Graciously.*) Please ladies. Stand on your four feet.

They do so.

Locksmith's Wife   A favour, your Excellency . . .

Sergeant's Widow   A favour . . .

Khlestakov   Who are you, anyway?

Sergeant's Widow   I'm Ivanova, the sergeant's widow.

Locksmith's Wife   Fevronya Poshlepkina, married to the locksmith . . .

Khlestakov   One at a time. What can I do for you?

Locksmith's Wife   It's the Governor. God rain His curses on the Governor and his wife and children. And his uncles and aunts, too.

Khlestakov   What's he done wrong?

Locksmith's Wife   He shaved my husband's head and sent him off into the army and it wasn't his turn and it's illegal because my husband is a married man.

Khlestakov   Then how can he do it?

Locksmith's Wife   He did it, he just did it! God punish him in this world and the next. May his aunt have convulsions, if he's got an aunt, and may his father choke to death if he's still alive! They should have taken the tailor's son, drunken little pig, but his parents made the Governor a beautiful overcoat, didn't they? So then he said he'd send the son of the draper but the draper sent three bolts of linen to the Governor's wife. So he comes round to me and he says, 'You don't need a husband like that,' he says, 'He's no bloody use to you.' Well, I'm the only one who knows if he's any use, aren't I? That's my business. Then he says, 'And your husband's a thief.' So I say 'He never stole anything.' So he says, 'Well, he's a potential thief. Prevention is better than cure. He's going in the army.' So I say, 'How can I live without that man, you old villain. I'm a weak defenceless woman! May all your relations get gangrene and if you've got a mother-in-law, may your mother-in-law –'

Khlestakov (*seeing her out*)   All right, all right.

Locksmith's Wife (*leaving*) Don't you forget, now.

Sergeant's Widow I came to complain about the Governor, sir.

Khlestakov Keep it short.

Sergeant's Widow He had me flogged, sir.

Khlestakov Really?

Sergeant's Widow By mistake, sir. Some women, fighting in the market. Police sent for. Got there too late. So they grabbed me and beat me and I couldn't sit down for two days.

Khlestakov Can't do much about that now.

Sergeant's Widow Not much. But it's against the law. You could fine him. I don't have much luck. A little compensation . . .

Khlestakov All right, all right, I'll do what I can. Out you go!

The **Sergeant's Widow** *goes, only pausing to wave at the window. This is greeted by cheering, and more petitions are thrown in.* **Khlestakov** *gathers them and throws them back.*

I've got enough to be going on with. No more. (*To* **Osip**.) I'm sick of these people. To hell with them. Don't let any more in. Osip!

Osip (*at the window*) Scram! Not now. Come back tomorrow. (*He shuts the window.*)

The curtains over the french windows billow out. **Khlestakov** *starts.*

Khlestakov What's that, Osip?

Osip *goes and flings back the curtains. The french windows are open. Through them is visible a white, endless landscape. A cold wind blows through the auditorium. Standing outside, in a group that seems to stretch to the horizon, are the very poor, men and women, children, babies, cripples, beggars etc.* **Khlestakov** *and* **Osip** *stare at them.*

Finally **Osip** *runs and slams the french windows and pulls the curtains closed after pushing out the nearest figure.*

Osip (*quietly and with some fear in his voice*)   Get out of here. Get away. Get away.

Enter **Marya**. *She sees* **Khlestakov**.

Marya   Oh!

Khlestakov   Don't be scared.

Marya   I'm not scared.

Khlestakov   I am delighted that you're not scared of me. Where are you off to then?

Marya   Well, I'm not off anywhere really.

Khlestakov   Why not?

Marya   I thought Mama was in here.

Khlestakov   I'm very interested in why you weren't off anywhere.

Marya   Ooh, I'm sorry. I disturbed you, didn't I? Important business, I suppose.

Khlestakov   Your eyes are more important than any business. As for disturbing me – such a disturbance is exquisitely pleasurable.

Marya   Do they all talk like that in St Petersburg?

Khlestakov   Only when inspired by a goddess! Make me happy by allowing me to rearrange this chair for you. Ah, but this chair is unworthy, a mere machine for sitting on. You deserve a throne!

Marya (*sitting down*)   It's quite comfy, thanks. I ought to be off, really.

Khlestakov   What a pretty scarf you're wearing, child.

Marya   You're making fun of me, aren't you?

Khlestakov   Would that I were that scarf, so I could

dangle round your delicate white neck.

Marya It's just a scarf . . . Funny weather we're having aren't we?

Khlestakov Oh, the movement of your lips as you talk about the weather!

Marya You do talk so nicely. Will you make up a poem about me?

Khlestakov No poem could do you justice.

Marya But I would like a poem. I could put it in my album.

Khlestakov What sort of poem would you like?

Marya A new one. Just for me.

Khlestakov *smiles indulgently. He paces around trying his best, muttering to himself.*

Khlestakov Let's see, Marya – see . . . career . . . drear . . . fear . . . rear . . . no, another approach.

He suddenly sings:
  Marya's like a red, red rose
  That's newly sprung in June.
  Marya's like the melody
  That's sweetly played in tune.
  So fair art thou, Marya-a,
  So deep in love am I,
  That I will love thee, Ma-ray-a
  Till all the seas go dry.

He sings fervently and beautifully, apart from his struggle to adapt the lyrics.

(*Speaks.*) Hm? I'll make up some more verses. But what's a song? A petal on the great black lake of time. (*He sits.*)

Marya Who said that?

Khlestakov I did. Instead of a song, I would rather offer you and proffer you the unstinted devotion and passionate love which the moons of your eyes have set fire to in my heart. (*He moves his chair nearer to her.*)

Marya   Love? I'm not sure that I know the meaning of the word. (*She moves her chair away.*)

Khlestakov (*moving closer*)   Don't move away. This is cosier, closer.

Marya (*moving away*)   Why so close? It's the same further away.

Khlestakov (*moving up*)   Why further away? It's the same nearer. The same only better.

Marya (*moving away*)   What are you up to?

Khlestakov   Please don't keep moving. You can pretend that we're hundreds of miles apart. (*He sighs.*) I'd be a happy man if I could only hold you in my arms.

Marya (*looking out of the window*)   Was that a magpie just flew past?

Khlestakov (*looking out and kissing her shoulder*)   Well, it was some sort of pie.

Marya (*standing up*)   Now stop it! You think just because I live in the provinces you can ... (*She tries to get away.*)

Khlestakov (*holding her*)   It's love, it's love! Please don't be angry, can't you take a joke? Please – I'd go down on my knees to ask your forgiveness – (*He suddenly kneels.*) – you see I have gone down on them. Did you hear that little cracking sound? (*He rubs his knee.*)

Enter **Anna**, *who sees him on his knees.*

Anna   For heaven's sake.

Khlestakov *stands up.*

Anna   What are you up to, young lady? What do you think you're doing?

Marya   Mama. I ...

Anna Go to your room! This moment. And stay there.

Exit **Marya**, *in tears.*

Khlestakov (*aside*) There's something about a mother . . .
You know, she's not bad at all. (*He falls on his knees.*) You
see before you a poor fool on fire with passion.

Anna What are you doing down there? Get up. Please
get up. The carpet hasn't been swept.

Khlestakov Oh no! I will stand on my knees and plead
with you to decide my sentence. Is it life? Or death?

Anna I'm sorry, but I'm not quite with you. Are you
asking if you can marry our Marya?

Khlestakov Ha! No. You are the one I love. My life
hangs by a string. If you won't crown my constant passion,
I am less worthy than the worms. With a heart in flames I
ask for your hand.

Anna But, if you don't mind my saying so, I'm as it
were, married already.

Khlestakov That's nothing! What is a dusty legal
certificate compared with a love that fate decreed? Love
laughs at lawyers! We'll fly away, under the canopy of
some friendly waterfall. Your hand, grant me your hand.

Marya *rushes in.*

Marya Mama, father says you've got to . . . Oh, Lord!

Anna What is it now? Dashing about like a scalded cat.
Carrying on like a three-year-old! Nobody'd take you for
eighteen. You need some maturity, my girl, you need some
maturity and some good manners and some sophistication
too.

Marya (*in tears*) Oh, Mama, I didn't think . . .

Anna That's your trouble, you never do. You're just like
that Lyapkin-Tyapkin girl – brain like a split pea and a
heart like a gooey pudding. Why can't you learn from your
betters? Like your mother?

Khlestakov (*taking* **Marya**'*s hand*)   Oh Mrs Skovznik-
Dmuchanovsky – don't oppose our happiness! Please give
your blessing to our never-ending love.

Anna (*dumbfounded*)   You mean it's her?

Khlestakov   Pronounce your sentence. Is it life, or death?

Anna   You see, you daft creature? For your sake our guest
went down on his knees to ask for your hand, and you
come rushing in like an inebriated Cossack. Serve you right
if I refused to give my consent.

Marya   Oh Mama, I'll never do it again. Promise.

Enter the **Governor**, *out of breath.*

Governor   Your Excellency! Please have mercy.

Khlestakov   What's up with you?

Governor   It's those merchants. I know they've been
complaining. I promise you, on my honour as a gentleman,
they're a gang of liars. Cheating the public, giving short
measure! And that story of the Sergeant's widow is an
absolute fabrication – she flogged herself.

Khlestakov   Oh, I don't give a damn about her.

Governor   Don't believe any of them. They're all liars!
They couldn't fool a child! They're the biggest cheats
between here and Barcelona.

Anna   My darling, Mr Khlestakov has done us a great
honour. He went down on his knees and asked if he could
marry our Marya.

Governor   Marry our Marya! You're out of your mind,
woman! Take no notice, your Excellency, it's the time of
the year, takes her like this, runs in the family. You should
see her mother!

Khlestakov   I'd quite like to. No. But it's true. I want to
marry Marya. You see – I love her.

Governor   It's unbelievable!

Khlestakov If you don't let me marry Marya, there's no telling what I'll do.

Anna He means it. He really means it.

Khlestakov Give her to me! Give me to her! Give us to each other! If I shoot myself, you'll be prosecuted! But perhaps you don't think I'm good enough? You're trying to break it to me gently! Right! I shall end my useless life. Can you lend me some rope?

Governor You misunderstand, your Excellency. Good enough for Marya? Too good for her, some might say. Of course I give my consent. Do whatever you like. My poor head! It's whizzing round and round. I feel a proper fool.

Anna Bless the happy couple, my dear.

Governor May God bless you and don't blame me.

Khlestakov *embraces* **Marya** *as the* **Governor** *looks on.*

Governor Good heavens, they're hugging each other! They're kissing! They're in love! They're engaged. I've done it. Three cheers for the Governor! (*Sobered up suddenly.*) What a turn-up for the book!

Enter **Osip**.

Osip The troika is ready.

Khlestakov Yes, yes . . . In a minute.

Governor What? Are you leaving us already?

Khlestakov Great shame. Must be off.

Governor But where are you going to . . . I mean, just a minute ago we were talking about something, a wedding wasn't it?

Khlestakov Er, that's right. But I've got to nip off for a minute, well just for a day. To see my uncle. He's a rich old man. Very rich. And very old. So I'd better hurry. And ask his blessing. Be back tomorrow.

Governor Oh, to ask his blessing and tell him the good

news. Well, we mustn't hold you up.

Khlestakov   Oh I'll be back before I've gone. Goodbye, my love – I can't express what I'm feeling. Goodbye, my darling! (*He embraces* **Marya**.) And Mother, goodbye! (*He hugs* **Anna**.)

Governor   Have you got everything you need for the journey? You were a little short of cash . . .

Khlestakov   Not any more. (*He considers*.) Yes, maybe.

Governor   How much would cover your expenses? You mustn't be out of pocket.

Khlestakov   Well, you lent me two hundred, no, four hundred – you made a mistake didn't you, but I'll not take advantage of that. Could you let me have the same again, make it a round eight hundred?

Governor (*handing over the money*)   There we are. Nice brand new notes.

Khlestakov (*counting and pocketing*)   There's nothing brings more good luck than a handful of crackling bank notes – as they say in St Pete's.

Governor   Very true. Shall we proceed to your troika?

The **Governor**, **Anna**, **Marya** *and* **Osip** *accompany* **Khlestakov** *out*.

Scene One And A Half

Outside: the troika, a magnificent sledge drawn by three fine horses awaits. Beside it stand the **Schools Superintendent**, *the* **Judge**, *the* **Charity Commissioner**, **Doctor Gibner**, **Dobchinsky** *and* **Bobchinsky** *plus various* **Merchants**. **Osip** *runs on and is followed by the* **Governor**, **Khlestakov**, **Anna** *and* **Marya**.

Khlestakov (*turning and taking* **Marya**'s *hands*)   Goodbye, my soul's angel, Marya! (*He grapples with her, then breaks away* *and steps into the troika.*)

Governor   I would like to present you with this Persian travelling rug.

Khlestakov (*snuggling down into it*)   So kind.

All   And please, your Excellency, accept . . .

*They all step forward and fill the troika with gifts for **Khlestakov**. These include a horse-collar, a cigar lighter, a silver ewer, a length of cloth, spectacular crockery, a large oil painting, a pair of boots, sword, a hookah and a barrel organ. **Khlestakov** reacts royally, but is most pleased when **Doctor Gibner** presents him with a little flask. He samples it and grins.*

Khlestakov   Auf Wiedersehn.

Governor   When can we expect you back, my son?

Khlestakov   Tomorrow. Maybe the day after.

Osip   Are you ready sir?

Khlestakov   I'm ready. Bye bye, Marya.

Governor   Goodbye, your Excellency.

Osip *cracks his whip. The waving officials are lost in the distance and all we see is the troika racing across the snow.*

Osip (*to the horses*)   Come on, you German clown! Get on with it! Look at the boy, he's a good old feller, that's why I give him extra feed, he does extra work. And the young one, too, he's a good horse, does his duty. But you just shake your ears like a fool. Come on! Ah – you can move when you want to – Gee up, my three beauties! Hey, you're not a bad little team!

Khlestakov   Faster, faster, the faster the finer, I love it, of course I do, I'm a Russian. Give the horses their heads. Let 'em go, and to hell with the world.
  Something's lifting me. I've got wings. I'm flying. And everything else is flying too, but flying the other way – milestones and wagons and forests and villages, all flying backwards, away from me. Faster.

Hey troika, you're fast as a bird. Troika, who invented you? Must have been a tough old people. Must have been a rough old country, a poor old country laying sprawled out over half the world.

Hey, troika, you, you're no fancy carriage. You're a wooden thunderbolt. You're hacked and cut and shaped and fitted with an axe and chisel by some hairy peasant, beard down to his boots. Faster.

And your horses, hey, they outgallop the wind. And the road smokes and shudders under you. And a soldier yells and stops to stare as you fly, fly, fly away till you're lost on the edge of nowhere, one black speck in a world of whiteness.

Hey, Russia, you're speeding like this troika.

What's your future, Russia, my amazing Russia? What's the force that drives your mystery horses? Their manes are rioting in the wind. Flying, flying on some God-given mission. Faster.

Where are you racing to, Russia? No answer, as usual, no answer. Just the odd shakey music of the horses' bells. Torn to a thousand tatters, the wind roars past you.

And now you're overtaking the whole world. And one day you'll make every country stand aside and stare as you pass. Every country, every empire – hey they'll all make way for you, Russia, they'll all make way for you.

The bells of the troika are heard after we lose sight of the troika.

Scene Two

The drawing room as in Act Two, Scene One.
The **Governor**, **Anna** *and* **Marya** *are in the room.*

Governor   Anna, my love, did you ever imagine anything like this? The wedding of the century! Come on, be frank, you never dreamed – one day the wife of a mere Police Governor and the next – hell's bells – to be married to such a dashing young devil!

Anna   What d'you mean? I saw it coming a mile off. Of

course it's a surprise to you, because of your
unsophistication. You never mingled with the elite.

Governor   Come on, Mother, I'm not that simple. But
Anna – we used to be sparrows and now we're eagles. Now
I know what a tadpole feels like when it suddenly changes
into a great big frog! And so those moaners and groaners
with their whingey petitions had better watch out! Because
it's bum-kicking time! (*He calls out of the door.*) Hey! Get in
here!

Enter **Constable Svistunov**.

Right, my lad. Go and fetch all those merchants. Complain
about me, would they? What a lovely little bunch of Judas
Iscariots! (*To the imaginary merchants.*) Just you wait – you
creepy-crawly creatures! I'm going to flatten the lot of you.
(*To* **Svistunov**.) I want a list of all the whiners. Get 'em all
down. And when you've finished the list, take a wander
round the town. And spread the news. Make sure everyone
knows that God has blessed the Governor. Tell 'em my
daughter's getting married, not to some scruffy little clerk,
but to a great man from Petersburg, a man like this town
has never seen, a man who can do anything, anything,
anything! Shout it aloud in the streets, ring the church bells
and to hell with it. When I celebrate, I bloody celebrate!
Give us the list and hop off!

Svistunov *hands over his list and leaves.*

Governor   Good. All right, my love, where do you feel
like living now? Here or Petersburg?

Anna   Oh, Petersburg, of course. There's nothing here.

Governor   Hmm . . . Well, Petersburg you say and
Petersburg it shall be. Though I'm quite fond of my own
little patch. Well, Anna, it looks like goodbye to my days as
Police Governor.

Anna   I should hope so. Who cares about governors?

Governor   Anyway, I should get a top job out of this,
don't you think Anna? Because he's friends with all those

ministers and he pops in and out of the palace, so he could maybe fix things, somehow, eventually, so that I could even be a general. D'you think I might get to be a general?

Anna   I should think so! You'd make a wonderful general.

Governor   Ohh, it's a nice feeling, being a general! I'll kneel and he'll place a sash around my shoulder. Which sash is better, Anna, the red or the blue?

Anna   Blue, of course.

Governor   You're an ambitious woman! I'd be happy with the red sash. You know, there's something about being a general – wherever you travel you've got special messengers galloping ahead of you, commandeering the best horses, the finest billets, the choicest food and wine. And all those little landowners and captains and governors – none of them gets a look in. Maybe you're having dinner with some prince and there – you're sitting there scoffing and some poor little provincial police governor has to stand and watch you. (*He explodes with laughter.*) It must be grand to be a general!

Anna   Scoffing? Anton, we must get your vulgarity seen to. Our whole way of life is going to have to change. And we'll be changing our friends, too. No more hearty judges stinking like kennels. No more shifty charity commissioners and certainly no more German doctors. No, your acquaintances will all be persons of refinement, counts, archdukes and so on. Oh, but Anton, I do worry about you. The things you come out with. Society people never use language.

Governor   What d'you mean? There's no harm in words.

Anna   You could say what you liked when you were just a governor. But in St Petersburg we're going to mix with civilised people.

Governor   I've heard that they serve two fish dishes – Carp à la Nevsky and eels in aspic, which are so delicious that your tongue curls up in delight . . .

Anna   Fish – that's all you care about! I want our house
to be the chicest in St Petersburg. I always dreamed of a
boudoir. My boudoir will be sprayed with so much French
scent that you'll have to screw up your eyes when you walk
in. (*She screws up her eyes and sniffs.*) Mmmmmmmmmm!
Lovely!

The **Merchants**, *looking very humble, are shown in.*

Governor   Ah! Hello, my little sweethearts!

Merchants (*bowing and, but not excessively, scraping*)   Good
health to you, your Excellency!

Governor   How are you, my dear friends? And how's
business? And so . . . you tea-swilling pedlars, you have
lodged a complaint? A complaint from the Ancient Order
of Cheats and Chisellers? You put water in the vodka, sand
in the sugar and toenails in the brawn. And you complain
about me? Aha, you thought, we'll get him put away,
didn't you? Well, now we'll sodding well see who's put
away –

Anna   Language, Anton, language!

Governor   Shut up, woman! Listen, insects! You know
that inspector you went crawling to? Well, he's going to
marry my daughter. Yes. What've you got to say to that? I
am going to show you. OOH! You sign a contract with the
government for army uniforms, clear a cool hundred
thousand by using rotten cloth, offer me point two per cent
and expect me to be grateful? Have you heard of Siberia?
And you push out your belly as if you're proud of it, as if
you're as good as an aristocrat. Well, you're not, because
an aristocrat, he learns something. He has it flogged into
him at school and he ends up knowing something useful.
But you? First day at work your master beats you because
you don't know how to swindle. And cheating is all you
ever learn. You're just a boy, you don't know the Lord's
Prayer, do you? But you know how to give short measure,
don't you? And you. If you're going to put on airs, you'd
better learn some manners. You'd better learn about

weights and measures, you'd better learn not to pester important people with bills and you'd better learn to grovel!

Merchants (*bowing*)   We are guilty, your Excellency!

Governor   And you complain about me? And who bailed you out when you built a bridge with a hundred roubles worth of timber and you claimed for twenty thousand? I pulled you out of the shit by your beard! Have you forgotten that? If it wasn't for me, you'd be shovelling salt!

1st Merchant   We are all guilty, your Excellency. The devil tempted us, and we fell! We promise never to do it again. Please forgive us!

Governor   Forgive you! I know why you're all whining to me now. Because I've got the lot of you by the short and curly. Because I've won. But if things had gone differently you'd have trampled me down into the mud and smashed me over the head with a tree-trunk.

Merchants (*bowing low*)   Please don't ruin us, your Excellency.

Governor   Don't ruin us! Don't ruin us, is it? Well, may God forgive you, I won't. But I'm not a man to bear a grudge. Only, look out, watch out! As your Governor, I would not be insulted if you were to congratulate me on my daughter's wedding. Tangible congratulations you understand. And not just a second-hand samovar and a couple of pounds of salted reindeer. Right. Now, get out of here – and God be with you.

The **Merchants** *leave.*
The **Judge** *and* **Charity Commissioner** *appear in the doorway, dressed up to the nines, smiling, bearing bouquets.*

Judge   Can one believe the rumours, Anton? Has the Goddess Fortune showered you with herrings, as my grandmother used to say?

Charity Commissioner   Tremendously pleased. Absolutely delighted. (*He kisses* **Anna***'s hand.*) Anna! (*He kisses* **Marya***'s hand.*) Marya!

Rastakovsky, *an ageing former official and a landowner with a voluminous beard, comes in, smiling, with a bouquet.*

Rastakovsky   My congratulations, young Anton! May the good Lord preserve your life and guard the young couple from all terrible dangers and grant you a multitude of unafflicted grandchildren and great grandchildren! Anna! Marya! (*More hand kissing.*)

Korobkin *and his* **Wife** *enter, they are very well dressed and sophisticated, obviously the local aristocrats.*

Korobkin   Congratulations, old man. We just popped round to wish all the best to the happy couple. Yes. May all their troubles be little ones, eh?

They are all convulsed by this amazing joke. **Korobkin** *and his* **Wife** *peck at the cheeks of* **Anna** *and* **Marya**.

Korobkin's Wife   We're absolutely transported with delight, my dear, absolutely transported!

More guests arrive, including **Bobchinsky** *and* **Dobchinsky** *with exactly similar bouquets.*

Bobchinsky   Congratulations all round.

Dobchinsky   Anton, I just wanted to say congratulations. It's really wonderful.

Bobchinsky   Oh, Mrs Skvoznik-Dmuchanovsky!

Dobchinsky   Oh, Mrs Skvoznik-Dmuchanovsky!

Both approach **Anna** *to kiss her cheeks but miss and bump heads.*

Marya! Congratulations all round! you'll be a fine lady now and wear a gown of gold and eat the most wonderful soup and have a really amusing life.

Bobchinsky   Marya! Congratulations all round! I hope you'll be very happy and rich with a whole stack of money and a baby boy so tiny he can sit in your hand, yes! (*He indicates the size.*) He'll be a real bouncing baby with a great big voice like this; 'Wah! wah! wah!'

Other guests arrive including the **Schools Superintendent** *and his* **Wife**.

Superintendent   I would just like to –

Superintendent's Wife (*hurrying to* **Anna**)   Congratulations, Anna. (*They kiss.*) I'm so happy for you! A little bird told me Anton's daughter is going to be married. 'Good heavens!' I said to myself. So I said to my husband, 'Listen Luka, Anna's had such a stroke of luck! I'm so pleased; I want to dash round and give her a kiss. I know she always wanted her daughter to marry well – it must be fate,' I said. I was overjoyed, I couldn't utter, oh I was crying with happiness! Sobbing my heart out! So Luka said, 'What are you crying about?' 'I don't know,' I said, 'The tears just came bursting out.'

Governor   Please sit down, ladies and gentlemen. Mishka, bring us some more chairs.

The **Police Inspector** *comes in with* **Constable Svistunov**.

Police Inspector   Well, I think congratulations are in order, sir.

Governor   Very kind, very kind.

Judge   I say, Anton, how did you clinch it?

Governor   Well, it was extraordinary. He proposed – of his own accord – just like that.

Anna   But he did it with so much tact and respect. He phrased it all so beautifully. He said to me: 'Anna, may I call you Anna? Your virtues enchant me.'

Marya   But, Mama!

Anna   That's enough from you! He's such a lovely, well brought-up gentleman. A man of principle. And so sincere! He said to me, he said 'Believe me, Anna, life means nothing to me. But I'm glad that I was born because now I have met you!'

Marya   But Mama, that's what he said to me!

Anna   Nonsense, Marya, you ignoramus. He spoke so
beautifully, a bit like that big monk from Georgia, and I
wanted to say: 'We're just an ordinary family, you know,'
but he fell on his knees and said, in a lovely deep voice;
'Anna, if you don't respond to my feelings, then life means
nothing to me. I shall finish my life in the only possible
way – by death!'

Marya   But Mama. He was saying all that about me.

Anna   Well, of course it was all about you. I'm not saying
it wasn't.

Governor   I was scared stiff, I don't mind admitting. He
kept on saying it 'I'll hang myself! I'll hang myself!'

Rastakovsky   Amazing! Amazing!

Judge   What a story!

Superintendent   Ah, but luckily, fate intervened!

Charity Commissioner   Not fate, old man – fate is
blind. It's just what our Governor deserved for all he's
done for this town. (*Aside.*) They do say that the biggest
pigs have the best luck.

Judge   Look, Anton, that pup you wanted. You can have
him, all right?

Governor   Thanks, but I haven't got time for dogs now.

Judge   Well, later, I'm sure we can find a dog that suits
you.

Korobkin's Wife   You can't imagine how thrilled I am
about your good luck, Anna.

Korobkin   Oh yes, by the way, where is your
distinguished guest? I heard that he's whizzed off.

Governor   Called away for a day or two, you know.
Urgent business.

Anna   To see his uncle, break the good news and ask for
his blessing.

Governor   That's right, to break the good news. But tomorrow . . .

The **Governor** *sneezes and everyone says 'Bless you' except* **Korobkin's Wife** *who says nothing and* **Korobkin** *who says 'Gesundheit'.*

Thank you. But he'll be back tomorrow.

The **Governor** *sneezes again. This time, among the 'Bless you's' and the single 'Gesundheit' can be heard the following.*

Police Inspector   Good health, your Excellency.

Bobchinsky   Live a hundred years and win a sack of gold.

Dobchinsky   God let you live one thousand six hundred years.

Charity Commissioner   Long may you rot!

Korobkin's Wife   Go to the devil!

Governor   Many thanks, my friends. And the same to you.

Anna   Of course we'll be moving to Petersburg. For the atmosphere more than anything – it's so provincial here! And of course, they'll probably make Anton a general.

Governor   Well, I admit it, gentlemen. I wouldn't mind being a general.

Superintendent   God knows I hope they make you one.

Rastakovsky   God moves in a mysterious way.

Judge   Won't be a big fish in a little pond, eh? You'll be . . . oh. (*He realises this isn't the right thing to say.*)

Charity Commissioner   A big fish in a big pond.

Judge (*aside*)   Make him a general. It's like putting a saddle on a cow! There's better men in this room who aren't generals yet.

Charity Commissioner (*aside*)   I suppose he could make a general. He's always acted like one. (*To the* **Governor**.) Ah, but you won't forget your old friends, will you Anton?

Judge   And you'll lend us a hand if there's ever any trouble, won't you?

Korbokin   I'm sending my son to Petersburg next year. Putting him for government service, you know. Wondered if you'd keep an eye on him, give him a leg up, you know?

Governor   I'll be very happy to do that.

Anna   Oh yes, Anton, you're very handy with your promises. You won't have any time for that sort of thing. Now don't start making promises to everyone who asks.

Governor   It'll be all right, my dear. One good turn . . . you know.

Anna   I know all right. But you don't want to start doing favours for a lot of nobodys.

Korbokin's Wife   You see what she thinks of us.

Superintendent's Wife   Oh, she's always been like that. You know what they say, 'Give a whore your old hat and she'll grab your tiara.'

Enter the **Postmaster** *with an opened letter in his hand.*

Postmaster   Ladies and gentlemen. Amazing news!

Governor   Out with it, then. We're all ears.

Postmaster   I don't know how to. It's such a shock. None of us ever dreamed.

All   Come on. What's the matter? What's in the letter?

Deciding to build up to the news, the **Postmaster** *gulps.*

Postmaster   Well, I was just going home when I came across a letter from the inspector we were showing round town. I looked at the address and it said 'Post Office Street.' I was dumbfounded. 'Well,' I thought, 'he's found something wrong in the work of my Post Office and he's reporting it to the authorities.' So I opened it.

Governor   How could you do that?

Postmaster   I don't know. As I stood there, dumbfounded, I seemed to hear a supernatural voice telling me to open the letter. Of course, I was horrified at the very idea. I put it down on the table and started to walk away for a glass of tea. But something seemed to pull me back to the table. I heard a voice in my right ear. 'Don't open it!' And then I heard another voice in my left ear saying, 'Come on! Open it!' One voice said, 'Don't open it! If you do, you're as dead as boiled chicken!' The other voice said, 'Don't be daft, open it! If you don't, you're as dead as a dumpling.' My hands felt as if they were metal being attracted by some giant magnet. I stood there, dumbfounded, for ten whole minutes. But in the end – I opened it.

Governor   How dare you?

Postmaster   I don't know. I've never been so scared in my life. I drew the curtains, locked the door and plugged the lock with a bit of chewed-up paper. And my samovar was boiling. And I picked up the envelope. And then the envelope felt as if it was red-hot. And when I steamed it open with the samovar, icy shivers ran up and down my back. And my front as well. Hot and cold sweat running down the inside of my uniform. My brain went all soggy. I didn't know where I was. My teeth were chattering so hard that it was a whole hour before I could read a line.

Governor   But how dare you interfere with the official correspondence of such an important person?

Postmaster   But that's just the point. He's not important and he's not a person. He's not from the government. And he's not an inspector.

Governor   (*unperturbed, quelling the others*)   All right, since you know so much, who is he?

Postmaster   He's nothing at all. God knows what he is.

Governor   What do you mean? Don't speak of him like

that. I'm putting you under arrest!

Postmaster You what? You?

Governor Yes! Me!

Postmaster You can't do that.

Governor Don't you know that he's going to marry my daughter so that I will be an important person and you will be packed off to Siberia?

Postmaster Siberia's a long way from home, as they say in the post office. But maybe I should read the letter. Would you like that?

All Come on. Read it. Get on with it.

Postmaster Well, it's addressed to Tryaptichkin, Journalist, Post Office Street, St Petersburg. And it says: 'My dear Tryaptichkin, in haste to let you know what I've been up to. I got taken to the cleaners at cards by an infantry captain. And I finally got stuck up here. And the inn-keeper wanted me thrown in jail. Then, suddenly, thanks to my Petersburg clothes and looks, everyone in this godforsaken town took me for a government inspector. Now I'm living in the Governor's house, having a good time, and I'm flirting like the devil with his wife and his daughter. My only problem is which one to pounce on first – the mother, I think, because she seems ready for anything. Remember how that baker took me by the collar and threw me in the gutter because I ate all those pies and told him to put them down on Queen Victoria's account? Well, times have changed. They've all been greasing my palm – but of course we always call it a loan. You've never seen such ridiculous people! You'd laugh yourself sick! They'd make great characters for your funny articles. Take the Governor here – he's thick as a brick.'

Governor Impossible. You're making it up as you go along.

Postmaster All right. Look.

Governor (*reads*) 'As thick as a brick.' It's absurd. You wrote this yourself.

Postmaster I couldn't write all that stuff.

Charity Commissioner & **Superintendent** Read some more!

Postmaster 'As thick as a brick.'

Governor Damn it! You don't have to keep reading that bit. It's bad enough without that.

Postmaster Mmmmmmmm. 'Thick as a brick. The Postmaster is a very nice man. He . . .' Can't read the writing here.

Governor Go on, read it.

Postmaster Oh, why bother?

Governor If it has to be read, read the whole bloody lot.

Charity Commissioner Allow me. (*He puts on spectacles and reads.*) 'The Postmaster looks and smells like an alcoholic nightwatchman with spots'.

Postmaster (*to audience*) He needs a good punch on the nose. That's all.

Charity Commissioner 'As for the Charity Commissioner . . .' Mmmmmmmm.

Korobkin What's the matter?

Charity Commissioner There's a sort of smudge. (*Under his breath.*) The bastard!

Korobkin Let me see. I've got very keen eyesight.

Charity Commissioner No, there's only a couple of lines smudgy.

Korobkin I can see. Let me read it.

Charity Commissioner I'll do it. After this sentence it's perfectly clear.

Postmaster   Oh, no you don't! Read every word of it. Let's have it all!

Charity Commissioner   All right. (*To* **Korobkin**.) That's where I got to. You read it.

All   No. Further back. Read the smudge.

Korobkin   'As for the Charity Commissioner – he looks just like a pig in a skull-cap.'

Charity Commissioner (*to the audience*)   I don't think that's funny. Whoever saw a pig in a skull-cap?

Korobkin   'The School Superintendent always stinks of onions.'

Superintendent (*to the audience*)   I have never placed an onion in my mouth.

Judge (*aside*)   Thank God there's nothing about me, anyway.

Korobkin   'While the Judge . . .'

Judge (*aside*)   There you are! (*Aloud.*) I think this letter's awfully long and boring. Why bother to read out all that rubbish?

Superintendent   Keep reading!

Charity Commissioner   Carry on!

Korobkin   'While the Judge is very, very mauvais ton.' – a French expression, you know.

Judge   Mauvais ton? Could mean anything. I don't mind if it just means stupid, but it might be something worse.

Korobkin   'On the whole, though, they're generous, warm-hearted folk. I'd better say goodbye, my dear Tryapichkin. I want to follow your example and go in for literature. Life's very dull if you don't have a hobby. So I think I'll write a novel or a play or something. Drop me a line in Saratov. Your old friend, Ivan Khlestakov.'

Korobkin's Wife   Oh, dear. How embarrassing.

Governor　He's murdered me, murdered me! The end, the end, it's the end of everything! I can't see anything. They aren't faces any more, they're snouts, pigs' snouts! Fetch him back! Fetch him back here!

Postmaster　How can we? We gave him the fastest troika in town.

Korobkin's Wife　It's really terribly awkward.

Judge　Oh, my God! I lent him three hundred roubles.

Charity Commissioner　Me too – three hundred roubles.

Postmaster (*sighing*)　And three hundred from me.

Bobchinsky　Dobchinsky and I gave him sixty-five between us . . .

Judge　How could we do it? How could we make such a bloomer?

Governor　How could I do it? How? I – I – I've been a bloody fool. Thirty years in local government – and not one merchant, not one contractor ever got the better of me, not one! I've cheated the cheats and swindled the swindlers. They went fishing for me but their hooks always ended up stuck through their own tongues. I've fooled three senior governors in succession. Not that senior governors know what goes on . . .

Anna　But it can't be true, Anton. I mean Marya's his fiancée.

Governor　Fiancée! Fiancée! Don't fling that silly word in my face! He's fiancéed off, hasn't he? Look! Everybody look! Roll up, roll up, all good Christians, the entire population of the world, roll up, roll up! See the biggest fool in the universe! (*He shakes his fist at himself.*) Oh you fat-faced idiot! To mistake that dimwitted little nothing for an important official! And now he's speeding across the landscape with all the troika bells ringing! He'll spread this story all over the world. They'll laugh at me, but that's not all. Some scribbler will write a comedy about it. That's what hurts. He'll put it all in. My position! My struggles! He'll show no mercy. And everyone will laugh and clap and . . . (*To the audience.*) What are you laughing at? You're laughing at yourselves! (*He stamps.*) These so-called writers. Dangerous liberals and inky thugs! I'd like to tie them up in a reef knot, grind them into flour and send them to the devil for a lining for his hat! What! (*Pauses.*) I can't think. Madness is a flogging from God, as my old nurse used to say. But how did this idea of a Government Inspector crawl into my brain? In the beginning, there was nothing. And then, suddenly everyone was saying it – 'An Inspector', 'Government Inspector', 'The Inspector's arrived.' Now who was it suggested that that young man was the Government Inspector? Who was it?

Charity Commissioner   For the life of me, I can't remember. It crept upon us like a fog, a fog from hell.

Superintendent   There was a letter . . .

Judge   Yes, a letter. Yesterday morning. And you called us here.

Governor   I know that. But who said *he* was the one.

Judge   Who said it first? They did, those two. (*He points at* **Bobchinsky** *and* **Dobchinsky**.)

Bobchinsky   Oh no! It wasn't me! I didn't think!

Dobchinsky   I did nothing! Nothing!

Superintendent   Of course it was them! They came sprinting over from the inn babbling away, 'He's arrived! He's here! He doesn't pay any money.'

Governor   It would be you two, wouldn't it? The town gossips, the local liars.

Charity Commissioner   To hell with you and your Inspector!

Governor   You chubby little snoopers! Blundering about all over the place creating panic, you bloody blabbermouths!

Judge   Hooligans!

Superintendent   Imbeciles!

Charity Commissioner   Pot-bellied shrimps!

Postmaster   Alcoholic piglets!

They all crowd round **Bobchinsky** *and* **Dobchinsky**.

Bobchinsky   It wasn't my fault! It was Dobchinsky!

Dobchinsky   No, Bobchinsky, you were the first one
to . . .

Bobchinsky   Honestly Dobchinsky, it was your
stomach . . .

The door flies open and a **Gendarme** *in a resplendent uniform,
quite different from the town police, stands there.*

Gendarme   The Government Inspector has arrived from
Saint Petersburg with orders from the Czar. He is staying
at the inn. And he wants to see all of you there,
immediately.

*There is a rolling thunderclap. All the ladies give an exclamation of
astonishment, as if by one person. The entire group shifts, suddenly
changing its position and then remaining frozen.*
   A tableau. The **Governor** *stands in the middle like a pillar
with outspread hands, his head thrown back. To the right are* **Anna**
and **Marya**, *in a posture as if rushing towards him. Behind them is
the* **Postmaster**, *who becomes a question mark turned to the
audience.*
   Behind him the **Schools Superintendent** *who looks lost in
a most innocent way.*
   *Behind him, at the very edge of the stage, three lady visitors lean on
each other with very satiric expressions on their faces, intended for the*
Governor's *family.*
   On the **Governor**'s *left, the* **Charity Commissioner**, *his
head slightly to one side, as if listening to something. Behind him the*
Judge *with outspread hands, squatting, almost on the floor and
making a movement with his lips as if to say, 'Here's a how d'ye*

do!' *Behind him,* **Korobkin**, *turning to the audience with one eye half closed and a sarcastic look at the* **Governor**. *Behind him, at the very edge of the stage,* **Bobchinsky** *and* **Dobchinsky**, *with hands outstretched towards each other, stand open-mouthed and staring. The rest of the guests simply remain like pillars. For almost one and a half minutes the frozen group keeps this position.*

Curtain.

Methuen Modern Plays
include work by

Jean Anouilh
John Arden
Margaretta D'Arcy
Peter Barnes
Sebastian Barry
Brendan Behan
Dermot Bolger
Edward Bond
Bertolt Brecht
Howard Brenton
Anthony Burgess
Simon Burke
Jim Cartwright
Caryl Churchill
Noël Coward
Lucinda Coxon
Sarah Daniels
Nick Darke
Nick Dear
Shelagh Delaney
David Edgar
David Eldridge
Dario Fo
Michael Frayn
John Godber
Paul Godfrey
David Greig
John Guare
Peter Handke
David Harrower
Jonathan Harvey
Iain Heggie
Declan Hughes
Terry Johnson
Sarah Kane
Charlotte Keatley
Barrie Keeffe
Howard Korder

Robert Lepage
Stephen Lowe
Doug Lucie
Martin McDonagh
John McGrath
Terrence McNally
David Mamet
Patrick Marber
Arthur Miller
Mtwa, Ngema & Simon
Tom Murphy
Phyllis Nagy
Peter Nichols
Joseph O'Connor
Joe Orton
Louise Page
Joe Penhall
Luigi Pirandello
Stephen Poliakoff
Franca Rame
Mark Ravenhill
Philip Ridley
Reginald Rose
David Rudkin
Willy Russell
Jean-Paul Sartre
Sam Shepard
Wole Soyinka
Shelagh Stephenson
C. P. Taylor
Theatre de Complicite
Theatre Workshop
Sue Townsend
Judy Upton
Timberlake Wertenbaker
Roy Williams
Victoria Wood

Methuen Contemporary Dramatists
include

Peter Barnes (three volumes)
Sebastian Barry
Dermot Bolger
Edward Bond (six volumes)
Howard Brenton
  (two volumes)
Richard Cameron
Jim Cartwright
Caryl Churchill (two volumes)
Sarah Daniels (two volumes)
Nick Darke
David Edgar (three volumes)
Ben Elton
Dario Fo (two volumes)
Michael Frayn (three volumes)
John Godber (two volumes)
Paul Godfrey
John Guare
Peter Handke
Jonathan Harvey
Declan Hughes
Terry Johnson (two volumes)
Sarah Kane
Bernard-Marie Koltès
David Lan
Bryony Lavery
Deborah Levy
Doug Lucie

David Mamet (three volumes)
Martin McDonagh
Duncan McLean
Anthony Minghella
  (two volumes)
Tom Murphy (four volumes)
Phyllis Nagy
Anthony Nielsen
Philip Osment
Louise Page
Stewart Parker (two volumes)
Joe Penhall
Stephen Poliakoff
  (three volumes)
Christina Reid
Philip Ridley
Willy Russell
Ntozake Shange
Sam Shepard (two volumes)
Wole Soyinka (two volumes)
David Storey (three volumes)
Sue Townsend
Michel Vinaver (two volumes)
Arnold Wesker (two volumes)
Michael Wilcox
David Wood (two volumes)
Victoria Wood

Methuen World Classics
include

Jean Anouilh (two volumes)
John Arden (two volumes)
Arden & D'Arcy
Brendan Behan
Aphra Behn
Bertolt Brecht (six volumes)
Büchner
Bulgakov
Calderón
Čapek
Anton Chekhov
Noël Coward (eight volumes)
Eduardo De Filippo
Max Frisch
John Galsworthy
Gogol
Gorky
Harley Granville Barker
  (two volumes)
Henrik Ibsen (six volumes)
Lorca (three volumes)

Marivaux
Mustapha Matura
David Mercer (two volumes)
Arthur Miller (five volumes)
Molière
Musset
Peter Nichols (two volumes)
Clifford Odets
Joe Orton
A. W. Pinero
Luigi Pirandello
Terence Rattigan
  (two volumes)
W. Somerset Maugham
  (two volumes)
August Strindberg
  (three volumes)
J. M. Synge
Ramón del Valle-Inclán
Frank Wedekind
Oscar Wilde

Methuen Student Editions

A SELECTED LIST OF METHUEN MODERN PLAYS

☐ CLOSER	Patrick Marber	£6.99
☐ THE BEAUTY QUEEN OF LEENANE	Martin McDonagh	£6.99
☐ A SKULL IN CONNEMARA	Martin McDonagh	£6.99
☐ THE LONESOME WEST	Martin McDonagh	£6.99
☐ THE CRIPPLE OF INISHMAAN	Martin McDonagh	£6.99
☐ THE STEWARD OF CHRISTENDOM	Sebastian Barry	£6.99
☐ SHOPPING AND F***ING	Mark Ravenhill	£6.99
☐ FAUST (FAUST IS DEAD)	Mark Ravenhill	£5.99
☐ COPENHAGEN	Michael Frayn	£6.99
☐ POLYGRAPH	Robert Lepage and Marie Brassard	£6.99
☐ BEAUTIFUL THING	Jonathan Harvey	£6.99
☐ MEMORY OF WATER & FIVE KINDS OF SILENCE	Shelagh Stephenson	£7.99
☐ WISHBONES	Lucinda Coxon	£6.99
☐ BONDAGERS & THE STRAW CHAIR	Sue Glover	£9.99
☐ SOME VOICES & PALE HORSE	Joe Penhall	£7.99
☐ KNIVES IN HENS	David Harrower	£6.99
☐ BOYS' LIFE & SEARCH AND DESTROY	Howard Korder	£8.99
☐ THE LIGHTS	Howard Korder	£6.99
☐ SERVING IT UP & A WEEK WITH TONY	David Eldridge	£8.99
☐ INSIDE TRADING	Malcolm Bradbury	£6.99
☐ MASTERCLASS	Terence McNally	£5.99
☐ EUROPE & THE ARCHITECT	David Grieg	£7.99
☐ BLUE MURDER	Peter Nichols	£6.99
☐ BLASTED & PHAEDRA'S LOVE	Sarah Kane	£7.99

• All Methuen Drama books are available through mail order or from your local bookshop.

Please send cheque/eurocheque/postal order (sterling only) Access, Visa, Mastercard, Diners Card, Switch or Amex.

☐☐☐☐☐☐☐☐☐☐☐☐☐☐☐☐

Expiry Date: _____ Signature: _____

Please allow 75 pence per book for post and packing U.K.

Overseas customers please allow £1.00 per copy for post and packing.

ALL ORDERS TO:

Methuen Books, Books by Post, TBS Limited, The Book Service, Colchester Road, Frating Green, Colchester, Essex CO7 7DW.

NAME: _____

ADDRESS: _____

_____

_____

Please allow 28 days for delivery. Please tick box if you do not wish to receive any additional information ☐

Prices and availability subject to change without notice.

For a complete catalogue of Methuen Drama titles
write to:

Methuen Drama
215 Vauxhall Bridge Road
London SW1V 1EJ

or you can visit our website at:

www.methuen.co.uk